$10.79/h.

11.25

$0.79

PAUL LITTLE

KNOW WHY YOU BELIEVE

NOW EXPANDED & UPDATED

by Marie Little

With Study Questions for Individuals or Groups

Illustrated by Joe DeVelasco
Foreword by Kenneth Kantzer

INTERVARSITY PRESS
DOWNERS GROVE, ILLINOIS 60515

InterVarsity Press is the book-publishing division of InterVarsity Christian Fellowship, a student movement active on campus at hundreds of universities, colleges and schools of nursing. For information about local and regional activities, write Public Relations Dept., InterVarsity Christian Fellowship, 6400 Schroeder Rd., P.O. Box 7895, Madison, WI 53707-7895.

All Scripture quotations, unless otherwise indicated, are from the Holy Bible, New International Version. Copyright © 1973, 1978, International Bible Society. Used by permission of Zondervan Bible Publishers.

Illustrated by Joe DeVelasco

ISBN 0-8308-1218-0

Printed in the United States of America

Library of Congress Cataloging in Publication Data

Little, Paul E.
   Know why you believe.

   Bibliography: p.
   1. Apologetics—20th century. I. Little, Marie.
II. Title.
BT1102.L5 1988   239   88-12810
ISBN 0-8308-1218-0

---

17   16   15   14   13   12   11   10   9
99   98   97   96   95   94

1 Is Christianity Rational? _____ 13

2 Is There a God? _____ 23

3 Is Christ God? _____ 39

4 Did Christ Rise from the Dead? _____ 49

5 Is the Bible God's Word? _____ 61

6 Are the Bible Documents Reliable? _____ 73

7 Does Archaeology Verify Scripture? _____ 85

8 Are Miracles Possible? _____ 101

9 Do Science and Scripture Agree? _____ 113

10 Why Does God Allow Suffering and Evil? _____ 131

11 Does Christianity Differ from Other World Religions? _____ 143

12 Is Christian Experience Valid? _____ 155

Notes _____ 169

Foreword

In my upper years of high school and first year of college I was searching for answers. I had lost my childhood faith and had found nothing to replace it. I needed a book like Paul Little's *Know Why You Believe*. His book came too late to help me, but eventually I found a group of Christian students, forerunners of InterVarsity Christian Fellowship. They knew what they believed and why they believed it, and met my need at the time.

For two decades now Paul Little's volume *Know Why You Believe* has served a similar purpose for several generations of students. Paul was neither a professional philosopher nor an historian. Strictly speaking, he was not a theologian. But he had a good mind and an amazing, almost intuitive understanding of people.

Considering the constant demands upon his time and energies, he read widely in apologetic literature; he possessed an uncanny sense for what was relevant. His friendliness, good will and spontaneous humor won him instant friends. Above all, his genuineness and his transparent personal integrity created a bond of trust with whomever he spoke—a lonely student in a university student union or a crowd of eager students during a widely advertised university mission.

Paul had no illusions that rational evidence could bring a person to genuine faith. Neither was he a "fideist" who thinks we must simply chose to believe irrespective of the evidence. In one sense you can't prove to anybody that Christianity is true. Yet it is possible to show good reasons why we ought to believe. Belief in Christ fits the facts infinitely better than unbelief.

Confident faith in Jesus Christ comes only as the Holy Spirit works in his mysterious ways to create a genuine faith. Yet the Spirit of God has used this volume by Paul Little to arouse faith in the hearts and minds of countless students. He has used it even more to confirm the faith of already committed Christians and to prepare them better to witness to others.

This is a good book. It presents the high-school, college or university student who is searching for the truth with facts he or she needs to know about the Christian faith.

Kenneth S. Kantzer
Chancellor of Trinity College
Deerfield, Illinois

Introduction

How This Book Began

This book has its roots in a university setting dating back to 1951 when my husband, Paul, was a new staff member with InterVarsity Christian Fellowship. He was scheduled to lead his first evangelistic discussion at the University of Kansas. Not only was this his first time to face a group of non-Christians alone, but it was to be in a Jewish scholarship hall. At the 6:00 P.M. dinner he would give a fifteen-minute introductory talk followed by questions from the men. He was terrified as he approached the hall. He often described his prayer to the Lord that day:

"Lord, you know I always stub my toe when I try to witness. Why must I begin in one of these residences reserved for brainy students on scholarships? They'll tear me apart limb from limb. I'll not live the night out!"

That night one man became a Christian, and years later his son became a missionary.

After Kansas Paul doggedly kept traveling from campus to campus, leading bull sessions and talking one-on-one to students. From hundreds of campuses on five continents, he sought to capture the attention of the bored, the intellectual, the athletic. He used clipped questions to jog their thinking and help the students to see flaws in scientific determinism and existentialism. He sprinkled in a few "sure-fire jokes" and other good humor. He'd say: "You exercised blind faith if you ate in a restaurant today." "Believing something doesn't make it true; refusing to believe it doesn't make it false." "Most people who say they don't believe the Bible have actually never read it."

In twenty-five years of lecturing, Paul found that regardless of which group he encountered there were twelve commonly asked questions. "They are predictable," he said. "If we think through the answers to the common questions we hear, we'll have the answers to the right questions. Right answers to the wrong questions aren't of much help!" From his own study of Scripture and his research of biblical scholars, he framed his answers. That's how *Know Why You Believe* was born.

The message of this newly edited book is entirely Paul's. I have changed the biblical references to the New International Version and updated illustrations in the specialized fields of archaeology and science in chapters two, seven and nine. The advice and additional material came from Paul's nephew Philip J. Ackley, Ed.D, Temple University; John H. Walton, Ph.D., Hebrew Union; David W. Suryk, J.D., Drake University; and Walter L. Liefeld, Ph.D., Columbia University. I am most grateful to each of them for their Christian generosity and expertise. Their contributions have significantly enhanced the value of Paul's succinct answers.

It has been thirteen years since that day when the dread news came of Paul's death in an auto accident. I am awed that the Holy Spirit has sovereignly chosen to continue the impact of his work. That this book has been read by more than a million people in the

United States and over thirty countries demonstrates how basic and universal are these questions. Paul would probably shake his head and say soberly, "This is God's work; the light comes from him." Without doubt this is why the book has been read so widely. Now with this updated edition, my earnest prayer is that each reader will be drawn to a deeper trust in the great God who speaks to both our minds and our hearts.

Marie Little
Prospect Heights, Illinois

1
Is Christianity Rational?

● ● ● ● ● ● ● ● ● ●

WHAT IS FAITH?" ASKED THE SUNDAY-SCHOOL TEACHER. A young boy answered in a flash, "Believing something you know isn't true."

That many non-Christians define faith this way is not surprising. That many believers overtly or secretly hold this view is tragic. For twenty-five years I've been asking this question in college and university bull sessions across the country. The average student of higher education will give the same answer as the boy. It may be couched in different terms, but the idea of self-deception and un-reliability will usually be there.

In these bull sessions I describe in simple terms what is the biblical definition of faith. Then I ask for questions from the floor. The responses are eye-opening.

Don't Kiss Your Brains Good-by

Unbelievers will say the session has been helpful because it's the first time they've heard a down-to-earth description of the Christian message. The convinced Christians will say they're relieved to discover that the gospel can be successfully defended in the open marketplace of ideas, and they haven't kissed their brains good-by in becoming Christians!

We live in an increasingly sophisticated and educated world. It is no longer enough to know what we believe. It is essential to know why we believe it. Believing something doesn't make it true. A thing is true or not regardless of whether anyone believes it. This is certainly true of Christianity.

There are two equally erroneous viewpoints abroad among Christians today on the important question of whether Christianity is rational. The first is, in essence, an anti-intellectual approach to Christianity. They misunderstand verses like Colossians 2:8: "See to it that no one takes you captive through hollow and deceptive philosophy, which depends on human tradition and the basic principles of this world rather than on Christ." Some use this verse in a way that gives the impression that Christianity is at least non-rational if not irrational. As a result these people fail to realize that a clearly reasoned presentation of the gospel "is important—not as a rational substitute for faith, but as a basis for faith; not as a replacement for the Spirit's working but as a means by which the objective truth of God's Word can be made clear so that men will heed it as the vehicle of the Spirit, who convicts the world through its message."[1]

There are challengers to our faith on every hand. Modern communications have made the world a neighborhood. We are likely to be challenged by Muslims, Hindus and Buddhists, all of them claiming valid religious experience that may approximate ours. From within Christendom we are now being told God is dead. Increasingly, in our scientific age, ethical humanism is having stronger appeal. Julian Huxley's *Religion without Revelation* is a good example of this approach.

The analytical philosopher Antony Flew states how meaningless to the non-Christian are religious assertions incapable of being tested objectively. He illustrates from a tale told by John Wisdom:

Once upon a time two explorers came upon a clearing in the jungle. In the clearing were growing many flowers and many weeds. One explorer says, "Some gardener must tend this plot." The other disagrees, "There is no gardener." So they pitch their tents and set a watch. No gardener is ever seen. "But perhaps he is an invisible gardener." So they set up a barbed wire fence. They electrify it. They patrol with bloodhounds. (For they remember how H. G. Wells' *The Invisible Man* could be both smelled and touched though he could not be seen.) But no shrieks ever suggest that some intruder has received a shock. No movements of the wire ever betray an invisible climber. The bloodhounds never give cry. Yet still the believer is not convinced. "But there is a gardener, invisible, insensible to electric shocks, a gardener who comes secretly to look after the garden which he loves." At last the skeptic despairs, "But what remains of your original assertion? Just how does what you call an invisible, intangible, eternally elusive gardener differ from an imaginary gardener or even from no gardener at all?"[2]

Evangelical scholar John Montgomery comments on this: "This parable is a damning judgment on all religious truth-claims save that of the Christian faith. For in Christianity we do not have merely an allegation that the garden of this world is tended by a loving Gardener; we have the actual, empirical entrance of the Gardener into the human scene in the person of Christ (Jn 20:14-15), and this entrance is verifiable by way of his resurrection."[3]

The opposite of the anti-intellectual approach comes from those who think that becoming a Christian is an exclusively rational process, that everything depends on the mind. Their tendency is to try to argue people into the kingdom. This is an impossibility and is as doomed to failure as attempting to put a hole in a brick wall by shooting it with a water pistol! There is an intellectual factor in the gospel, but there are also moral considerations. "The man without the Spirit does not accept the things that come from the Spirit of God, for they are foolishness to him, and he cannot understand them, because they are spiritually discerned" (1 Cor 2:14). Apart from the work of the Holy Spirit, no one will believe. But one of the instruments the Holy Spirit uses to bring enlightenment is a reasonable explanation of the gospel.

Know Some Answers

Beyond these pragmatic considerations, however, are the biblical assertions of the reasonableness of the gospel. Along with this there are clear biblical commands to Christians to be intelligent in their faith: "Always be prepared to give an answer to everyone who asks you to give the reason for the hope that you have" (1 Pet 3:15). If we are unable to give reasons for our faith, and if we allow the same questions to defeat us in conversation time after time, we are being disobedient. By our own ignorance, we are confirming unbelievers in their unbelief.

There are sound, practical reasons why this command has been given us. In the first place, it is necessary for the strengthening of our faith as Christians. If we know Jesus lives only because, as the hymn says, "he lives within my heart," we're going to be in trouble the first time we don't feel he's there. And when someone from a non-Christian position claims to have experienced the same thing from his god, our mouths will be stopped. We may choose to ignore doubts, but eventually they will "get to us." We cannot drive ourselves indefinitely by willpower to believe something of which we are not intellectually convinced. In fact, when someone tells us the only reason we believe is because of our parents and our religious background, we must be able to show ourselves and others that what we believe is objectively true, regardless of who told us.

A Rational Body of Truth

Many non-Christians fail to consider the gospel seriously because no one has ever presented the facts to them cogently. They associate faith with superstition based primarily on emotional considerations, and therefore they reject it.

Further biblical indication of the rational basis of the gospel appears in our Lord's command to "love the Lord your God with all your heart . . . and with all your mind" (Mt 22:37). The whole person is involved in conversion—the mind, the emotions and the will. Paul described himself as "defending and confirming the gospel" in Philippians 1:7. All of this implies a clearly understandable gospel which can be rationally understood and supported.

It is quite true that an unenlightened mind cannot come to the truth of God unaided, but enlightenment brings comprehension of a *rational body of truth.*

The gospel is always equated with truth. Truth is always the opposite of error (2 Thess 2:11-12). Non-Christians are defined by Paul as those who "reject the truth" (Rom 2:8). These statements would be meaningless unless there were a way to establish objectively what the truth is. If there were no such possibility, truth and error would, for all practical purposes, be the same because we would have no way to tell one from the other.

In writing to the Romans, the apostle Paul makes it clear that people have enough knowledge from creation itself to know there is a God (Rom 1:20). He goes on to show that the basic reason people do not know God is not because he cannot be known or understood but because human beings have rebelled against him, their Creator. "Although they knew God, they neither glorified him as God nor gave thanks to him (1:21) . . . and exchanged the glory of the immortal God for images made to look like mortal man (1:23). . . . They exchanged the truth of God for a lie" (1:25) and finally, they "did not think it worthwhile to retain the knowledge of God" (1:28).

Moral Smoke Screens

The moral issue always overshadows the intellectual issue in Christianity. It is not that people cannot believe—it is that he "will not believe." Jesus pointed the Pharisees to this as the root of the problem. "You refuse to come to me," he told them, "to have life" (Jn 5:40). He makes it abundantly clear that moral commitment leads to a solution of the intellectual problem. "If anyone chooses to do God's will, he will find out whether my teaching comes from God or whether I speak on my own" (Jn 7:17). Alleged intellectual problems are often a smoke screen covering moral rebellion.

A student once told me I had satisfactorily answered all his questions. "Are you going to become a Christian?" I asked.

"No," he replied.

Puzzled, I asked, "Why not?"

He admitted, "Frankly, because it would mess up the way I'm living." He realized that the real issue for him was not intellectual but moral.

The question is often asked, "If Christianity is rational and true, why is it that most educated people don't believe it?" The answer is simple. They don't believe it for the same reason that most uneducated people don't believe it. They don't want to believe it. It's not a matter of brain power, for there are outstanding Christians in every field of the arts and sciences. It is primarily a matter of the will.

John Stott struck a balance when he said, "We cannot pander to a man's intellectual arrogance, but we must cater to his intellectual integrity."

Doubt Strikes Terror

Sometimes Christians question their faith and even wonder if it's true. Doubt is a word that strikes terror to the soul and could be suppressed in an unhealthy way. This is a particularly acute problem for those who have been reared in Christian homes and in the Christian church. From their earliest years they have accepted the facts of Christianity solely on the basis of confidence and trust in parents, friends and minister. As the educational process develops, a reexamination of their position takes place.

This is a healthy and necessary experience to bring virile faith into being. It's nothing to fear or to be shocked about. Occasionally I ask myself, as I walk down the street, "Little, how do you know you haven't been taken in by a colossal propaganda program? After all, you can't see God, touch him, taste him or feel him." And then I go on to ask myself how I know the gospel is true. I always come back to two basic factors: the objective, external, historical facts of the resurrection, and the subjective, internal, personal experience of Christ that I have known.

When young people begin to question and appear to have doubts, they should be welcomed into a climate where they are free to "unload" and express their doubts. Many such young people have been driven underground and lost to the cause of Christ because the adults with whom they first talked had a high shock index. They implied that a good Christian would never doubt and that the questioner's spiritual life must be slipping because he or she was thinking. Young people aren't stupid. When they meet this response they quickly shift gears and mouth the party line, even though it doesn't come from the heart. They quietly wait until they are out from under pressure to conform, and then they shed a faith that had never become their very own.

Doubt and questioning are normal to any thinking person. Rather than express shock, it is better for us to hear the questioner out and, if possible, even sharpen the question a little more. Then an answer can be suggested. Because Christianity is about the one who is Truth, scrutiny will not harm it.

Don't Hit the Panic Button

If we don't have the answer at the moment, we needn't hit the panic button. We can always suggest we'll be glad to get the answer. It is improbable that anyone thought up, last week, the question that will bring Christianity crashing down. Brilliant minds have thought through the profound questions of every age and have ably answered them.

We don't have full answers to every question because the Lord hasn't fully revealed his mind to us on everything. "The secret things belong to the LORD our God, but the things revealed belong to us and to our children forever" (Deut 29:29). We possess enough information, however, to have a solid foundation under our faith. Christianity is based on evidence. It is reasonable faith. Christian faith goes beyond reason, but not against it.

Despite these facts, many Christians are overwhelmed by a mountain of material which they erroneously think they must master if they are ever to answer the questions of thinking Christians and non-Christians. A little exposure to non-Christians, however, will help to dispel those fears. It will soon become apparent that the same few questions are being asked repeatedly. Further, these questions fall within a remarkably limited range. In the college and university setting the audience may be composed of ninety-eight per cent non-Christians. It is possible for me to predict with a high degree of accuracy the questions that will be asked in the course of a half-hour question period. The questions may vary in wording, but the underlying issues are the same. This consistency is a great help to me in knowing what to study to answer such questions.

A Doubter's Response

A doubter needs to see that he must come to a decision after having been given an answer. To make no decision is to decide against the Christian position. Continued doubt in the face of adequate information may indicate an unwillingness to believe, and this may be a result of the questioner's will having been set against God.

Recently a friend told of a time, after he had finished college, when he felt God was calling him to the mission field. He fought against the call by feigning intellectual problems concerning his faith, rather than by praying clearly about his unwillingness to go overseas.

This book in intended to spotlight commonly asked questions and to suggest at least preliminary answers.

For the strengthening of our own faith and for the help of others, we must be ready to give an answer to everyone who asks us a reason for the hope that is within us, for Christianity is rational!

For Individual or Group Study

1. Centuries ago a person's faith in God was rarely challenged. Churches did almost nothing to encourage individuals to develop personal relationships with Christ. The church even withheld the Bible from popular use. Today society often views a person's faith in God as a relic of the past. Yet Christians have more resources than ever before to help them develop a personal faith in Christ— millions of Bibles, thousands of churches and hundreds of religious radio and television programs. Do you think it is harder or easier to have a genuine, growing relationship with Christ now than it was in earlier centuries? Explain.

2. "We live in an increasingly sophisticated and educated world" (p. 14). ". . . There are challenges to our faith on every hand" (p. 14). How, specifically, do you feel your world challenges your faith?

3. According to 1 Peter 3:15, we should "Always be prepared to give an answer to everyone who asks you to give the reason for the hope that you have. But do this with gentleness and respect." Why would the Bible include such a command?

4. How would obeying this verse help to dispel the faulty concept in nonbe-lievers' minds that faith is "believing something you know isn't true" (p. 13)?

5. "Alleged intellectual problems are often a smoke screen covering moral rebellion" (p. 18). Do you agree or disagree? Why?

6. Because it would be easy to lump all skeptics into the category of morally

rebellious smoke screeners, John Stott qualifies, "We cannot pander to a man's intellectual arrogance, but we must cater to his intellectual integrity" (p. 18). How would heeding this caution help a Christian treat each skeptic fairly and helpfully?

7. How do other factors (such as an abusive earthly father figure or emotional scars) affect one's ability to trust in God?

8. How are doubting Christians and skeptics usually handled in your fellowship group?

9. What is your usual response to the doubts of others—especially Christians who have professed faith for some time?

10. Is there a group in your church in which "doubters" can discuss their problems in an unhurried, nonthreatening way?

If not, and you think such a group would be of value, how could you help get one started?

11. Think of someone who genuinely seems open to trusting Christ yet is still having a problem believing. What reasons might cause this?

How could you help the person through the roadblocks?

12. "Apart from the work of the Holy Spirit, no one will believe" (p. 16). Pray now for the Holy Spirit's perspective on your friend's situation and for the Spirit's intervention.

13. Peter's encouragement to us to be prepared to give an answer for the hope that is in us is worth following through on. So as you work your way through this book, take time to compile a list of such reasons. You can start with any you have found in the course of reading this chapter. Space is provided for you following page 173.

For Further Reading

Chapman, Colin. *The Case for Christianity*. Grand Rapids, Mich.: Eerdmans, 1974.
Guinness, Os. *In Two Minds*. Downers Grove, Ill.: InterVarsity Press, 1976.
Purtill, Richard. *Reason to Believe*. Grand Rapids, Mich.: Eerdmans, 1984.

2
Is There a God?

● ● ● ● ● ● ● ● ● ●

T HERE IS IN HUMAN EXISTENCE NO MORE PROFOUND QUESTION
demanding an answer. Is there a God? is the question that must
be answered by every human being, and the answer is far-reaching
in its implications for every individual.

Mortimer Adler, in his monumental *Great Ideas Syntopicon,* an
essay on God, says: "With the exception of certain mathematicians
and physicists, all the authors of the 'Great Books' are represented
in this chapter. In sheer quantity of references, as well as in variety,
it is the largest chapter. The reason is obvious. More consequences
for thought and action follow the affirmation or denial of God than
from answering any other basic question."

Adler goes on to spell out the practical implications: The whole
tenor of human life is affected by whether people regard themselves
as supreme beings in the universe or acknowledge a superhuman

being whom they conceive of as an object of fear or love, a force to be defied or a Lord to be obeyed. Among those who acknowledge a divinity, it matters greatly whether the divine is represented merely by the concept of God—the object of philosophical speculation—or by the living God whom people worship in all the acts of piety which comprise the rituals of religion.[1]

God in a Test Tube?

We must be clear from the outset that it is not possible to put God in a test tube or prove him by the usual scientific methodology. And it can be said with equal emphasis that it is not possible to prove Napoleon by the scientific method. The reason lies in the nature of history itself, and in the limitations of the scientific method. In order for something to be proved by the scientific method, it must be repeatable. One cannot announce a new finding to the world on the basis of a single experiment. But history in its very nature is nonrepeatable. No one can rerun the beginning of the universe or bring Napoleon back or repeat the assassination of Lincoln or the crucifixion of Jesus Christ. But the fact that these events can't be proved by repetition does not disprove their reality as events.

There are many real things outside the scope of verification by the scientific method. The scientific method is useful only with measurable things. No one has ever seen three feet of love or two pounds of justice, but one would be foolish indeed to deny their reality. To insist that God be proved by the scientific method is like insisting that a telephone be used to measure radioactivity.

What evidence is there for God? It is very significant that anthropological research has indicated that among the farthest and most remote primitive peoples today, there is a universal belief in God. And in the earliest histories and legends of peoples all around the world the original concept was of one God, who was the Creator. An original high God seems once to have been in their consciousness even in those societies which are today polytheistic. This research, in the last fifty years, has challenged the evolutionary concept of the development of religion, which had suggested that monotheism—the concept of one God—was the apex of a gradual development that began with polytheistic concepts. It is increasingly clear that the oldest traditions everywhere were of one supreme God.[2]

The writer of Ecclesiastes referred to God as having "set eternity in the hearts of men" (Eccles 3:11). This was described by Blaise Pascal, the great seventeenth-century mathematician, as "the God-shaped vacuum" in every man. And Augustine concluded, "Our hearts are restless until they rest in thee."

For our present purposes, however, it is enough to observe that the vast majority of humanity, at all times and in all places, has believed in some kind of god or gods. Though this fact is not conclusive proof, by any means, we should keep it in mind as we attempt to answer the big question.

Law of Cause and Effect

To begin with, there is the law of cause and effect to consider. No effect can be produced without a cause. We as human beings, and the universe itself, are effects which must have had a cause. We come eventually to an uncaused cause, who is God.

Bertrand Russell makes an astounding statement in his *Why I Am Not a Christian.* He says that when he was a child, "God" was given him as the answer to the many questions he raised about existence. In desperation he asked, "Well, who created God?" When no answer was forthcoming, he says, "My entire faith collapsed!" But how foolish that was. God by definition is eternal and uncreated. Were God a created being, he would not and could not be God.

R. C. Sproul, author and lecturer, explains, "Being eternal, God is not an effect. Since he is not an effect he does not require a cause. He is uncaused. It is important to note the difference between an uncaused, self-existent eternal being and an effect that causes itself through self-creation!"[3]

Infinite Time Plus Chance?

No one would think a computer could come into being without an intelligent designer. It is unlikely that a monkey in a print shop could set Lincoln's Gettysburg Address in type. If we found a copy of it, we would conclude that an intelligent mind was the only possible explanation for the printing. How much more incredible is it to believe that the universe, in its infinite complexity, could have happened by chance? The human body, for instance, is an admittedly astounding and complex organism, a continual marvel of organization, design and efficiency. So impressed was Albert Einstein with this that he said: "My religion consists of a humble admiration of the illuminant superior Spirit who reveals himself in the slight details we are able to perceive with our frail and feeble minds. That deeply emotional conviction of the presence of a superior reasoning power, which is revealed in the incomprehensible universe, forms my idea of God."[4]

There are basically two choices for Christians and non-Christians alike: Did the universe begin by chance or by purpose and design? Scientists have long relied on infinite time plus chance to explain the origin of the universe and thus for them avoid the unacceptable conclusion of divine cause. They projected that given an ideally prepared primordial soup, jolted by frequent electrical charges and an unlimited period of time, some life form would evolve. However, the difficulties this theory presents are so enormous that today those same scientists are pointing out its weaknesses. The distinguished astronomer Sir Fred Hoyle has proposed an analogy to illustrate these difficulties. He asks, "How long would it take a blindfolded person to solve a Rubik's Cube?" If he made one move per second, without resting, he estimates it would take an astonishing 1.35 trillion years! Therefore, he concludes, when you consider the life expectancy of a human being, a blindfolded person could not solve the Rubik's Cube.

Hoyle then explains that it would be equally as difficult for the accidental formation of only one of the many chains of amino acids in a living cell. And in every human cell there are about 200,000 such amino acids. Now if you would compute the time required to get all 200,000 amino acids for one human cell to come together by chance, it would be about 293.5 times the estimated age of the earth (set at the standard 4.6 billion years). The odds against this happening would be infinitesimally small, far greater than a blindfolded person trying to solve the Rubik's Cube!

In another analogy Hoyle bolsters his argument. He calls this the "junkyard mentality" and asks, "What are the chances that a tornado might blow through a junkyard containing all the parts of a 747, accidentally assemble them into a plane, and leave it ready for take-off?" Hoyle answers, "The possibilities are so small as to be negligible even if a tornado were to blow through enough junkyards to fill the whole universe!"

In his impressive book *The Intelligent Universe,* Hoyle concludes, "As biochemists discover more and more about the awesome complexity of life, it is apparent that its chances of originating by accident are so minute that they can be completely ruled out. Life cannot have arisen by chance."[5]

Order and Design in the Universe

When we speak of design as opposed to chance we must look beyond the observable parts of our world, beyond the smallest of neutrons and protons, beyond the vastness of the galaxies. Rather, we need to ask who or what gave the original specifications and information that put it all together. This information is what we mean by design. It would be comparable to looking for the master plan that took glass, metal and phosphor and formed these parts into a functioning TV. No one would think of suggesting that "natural selection" or self-assembly produced such a product. Indeed, the term "natural selection" would not be an explanation, it would only be a label. It would not tell us how these parts knew enough to form together for a useful end. Someone had the information that programmed those parts into a TV.

In the same way the physical systems of our universe loudly proclaim that someone programmed the instructions into the individual parts to produce the world we see. Dr. Robert Gange suggests it would be valid to say that it was intentionally designed. If someone should claim that living structures can be traced to the physical properties of subnuclear particles, we still need to ask, "How did they arise?" Why, for example, does an electron have exactly the electrical charge and mass that it does? Why is it that light travels at precisely the speed it does? And who or what dialed the value of the gravitational "constant"?[6]

From the myriad examples we could cite of intentional design, consider the remarkable properties of plain water. Dr. L. J. Henderson enumerates some of these properties:

Water has a high specific heat. This means that chemical reactions within the [human] body will be kept rather stable. If water had a low specific heat we would "boil over" with the least activity. If we raise the temperature of a solution by ten degrees Centigrade we speed up the reaction by two. Without this particular property of water, life would hardly be possible. The ocean is the world's thermostat. It takes a large loss of heat for water to pass from liquid to ice, and for water to become steam quite an intake of energy is required. Hence the ocean is a cushion against the heat of the sun and the freezing blast of the winter. Unless the temperatures of the earth's surface were modulated by the ocean and kept within certain limits, life would either be cooked to death or frozen to death.

Water is the universal solvent. It dissolves acids, bases and salts. Chemically it is relatively inert, providing a medium for reactions without partaking in them. In the bloodstream it holds in solution the minimum of sixty-four substances. . . . Any other solvent would be a pure sludge. Without the peculiar properties of water, life as we know it would be impossible.[7]

The earth itself is evidence of design. "If it were much smaller an atmosphere would be impossible (as on Mercury and the moon); if much larger the atmosphere would contain free hydrogen (as on Jupiter and Saturn). Its distance from the sun is correct—even a small change would make it too hot or too cold. Our moon, probably responsible for the continents and ocean basins, is unique in our solar system and seems to have originated in a way quite different from the other relatively much smaller moons. The tilt of the [earth's] axis insures the seasons, and so on."[8]

Equally amazing examples of design can be seen within living things, including humans. There are approximately 11 million species of life on earth and each one is a living miracle. They are the result of mindboggling organizational intricacies at the molecular level that leave us in awe. Consider the human eye. The English theologian William Paley pointed to the "fitting together efficiently and cooperatively of the lens, retina and brain; enabling humans to have vision; as conclusive evidence of the design of an all-wise Creator. Thus the functional design of organisms and their features are taken as evidence of the existence of the designer."

Even Darwin himself in a chapter titled "Difficulties with the Theory" from his *Origins of Species* states, "To suppose that the eye, with so many parts all working together . . . could have been formed by natural selection, seems, I freely confess, absurd in the highest degree."

Harvard's Richard Lewontin, an evolutionist, states that organisms "appear to have been carefully and artfully designed" and calls the perfection of organisms "the chief evidence of a Supreme Designer."[9]

The Universe Had a Beginning

In addition to design in the universe, there is the implication that the universe had in some sense a beginning—a moment in time that brought the world into being. The Bible describes it this way: "In the beginning you [Lord] laid the foundations of the earth, and the heavens are the work of your hands" (Ps 102:25).

Scientists avoided the idea that time had a beginning or an end since it suggested divine intervention. Through the years a number of alternative theories were developed. One attempt was the "continuous creation/steady-state" model of the universe proposed in 1948 by Hermann Bondi, Fred Hoyle and Tom Gold. Dr. James Brooks, in his book *Origins of Life,* describes the model this way: "In the steady-state model, it was proposed that as the galaxies moved farther away from each other, new galaxies were formed in between, out of matter that was being 'continually created.' The universe would therefore look more or less the same at all times and its density would be roughly constant. The model suggests that matter (in the form of hydrogen) is always being created from nothing, and that this happens in order to counteract the dilution of material which occurs as the galaxies drift away from each other."[10] His conclusion from this and other factors is that the universe had no beginning and is eternal.

Dr. Robert Jastrow, founder of NASA's Institute for Space Studies, explains that the opposite is true. The moment a star is born it begins to consume some of the hydrogen in the universe, and there is a continual dilution of both hydrogen and the heavier metals in the universe today. He concludes that the theory of an eternal universe is untenable.[11]

A second explanation posed by scientists for the beginning of the universe has been called the "oscillating model." This says that the universe is like a spring, expanding and contracting, repeating the cycle indefinitely. The basis of this theory is that the universe is "closed," that is, no new energy is being put into it. The expansion of matter would reach a certain point and the force of gravity pull everything together before expanding again. However, all the evidence refutes this position; the universe is clearly losing density with no sign that the persistent expansion ever has or ever will reverse, and thus is not closed.

Dr. William L. Craig gives his conclusions about these two models with: "Both the steady state and oscillating models of the universe fail to fit the facts of observational cosmology. Therefore we can conclude once more that the universe began to exist."[12]

A third view of the beginning of the universe became known as the "Big Bang" theory. Dr. Edwin Hubble plotted the speeds of the galaxies and confirmed that all the galaxies are moving apart from us and one another at enormous speeds. The law bearing his name states: The farther away a galaxy is, the faster it moves.

The staggering implication of this is that at one time all matter was packed into a dense mass at temperatures of many trillions of degrees. Scientists who observed this phenomenon theorized that the universe must have originally resembled a white-hot fireball in the very first moments after the Big Bang occurred.

A confirmation of this theory came in 1965 when two physicists discovered that the earth was entirely bathed in a faint glow of radiation. Its waves followed the exact pattern of wavelength expected in a giant explosion. Scientists declared there could be no other obvious explanation than they were the aftermath of the Big Bang.

Dr. Robert Jastrow, who states that he is an agnostic in religious matters, comments on the theory of the Big Bang:

Now we see how the astronomical evidence leads to a biblical view of the origin of the world. The details differ, but the essential elements in the astronomical and biblical accounts of Genesis are the same. The chain of events leading to man commenced suddenly and sharply at a definite moment in time, in a flash of light and energy.

Scientists cannot bear the thought of a natural phenomenon which cannot be explained, even with unlimited time and money. There is a kind of religion in science; every event can be explained in a rational way as the product of some previous event; every effect must have its cause. Now science has proven that the universe exploded into being at a certain moment. It asks, "What cause produced this effect? Who or what put the matter and energy into the universe?" And science cannot answer these questions.

This is an exceedingly strange development, unexpected by all but the theologians. They have always accepted the word of the Bible. In the beginning God created heaven and earth. To which St. Augustine added, "Who can understand this mystery or explain it to others?"

He concludes with this monumental statement: "For the scientist who has lived by his faith in the power of reason, the story ends like a bad dream. He has scaled the mountains of ignorance; he is about to conquer the highest peak; as he pulls himself over the final rock, he is greeted by a band of theologians who have been sitting there for centuries."[12]

One of those theologians, David, said knowingly, "The heavens declare the glory of God; the skies proclaim the work of his hands" (Ps 19:1). And the apostle Paul wrote, "God has made it plain. . . . For since the creation of the world God's invisible qualities—his eternal power and divine nature—have been clearly seen, being understood from what has been made, so that men are without excuse" (Rom 1:19-20).

The Moral Argument
Yet another evidence for the existence of God is what C. S. Lewis calls "right and wrong as a clue to the meaning of the universe." There is an influence or a command inside each of us trying to get us to behave in a certain way. Lewis explains that universally we

find that people appeal to some sense of right and wrong. People argue with one another: "That's my seat. I had it first! Suppose I did the same to you! How would you like it? Come on, you promised. . . ." People say things like this every day, educated as well as uneducated, children as well as grown-ups; all of us say these things.

In these arguments there is an appeal to some behavioral standard that the other person is assumed to accept. He had a good reason to do it, it was okay to do it. The appeal is to some law or rule of fair play or morality that's built in them both. Rarely does the other person say, "Who cares about your standard?" It is there between them. They don't question it. As Lewis puts it, "Quarreling means trying to show the other man is in the wrong."

This law has to do with what ought to take place. Somehow we know it inside of us. It is not just a set of cultural norms or cultural standards. Also we can see there is a surprising consensus from civilization to civilization about what is moral decency. And we all do agree that some moralities are better than others. "If no set of moral ideas were truer or better than any other, there would be no sense in preferring civilized morality to savage morality, or Christian morality to Nazi morality."

Lewis says that the moral law cannot be merely a social convention. It is more like a mathematical table, he tells us. We would never say the math table is a social convention made up to help us and which we could have made differently if we wanted to. Two plus two will always equal four irrespective of its culture.

Yes, there is Somebody behind the universe. He has put a moral law within us and he is intensely interested in right conduct—in fair play, unselfishness, courage, good faith, honesty and truthfulness.

God—A Celestial Killjoy?

It is important to observe here that though there are many indications of God in nature, we could never know conclusively from nature that he exists or what he is like. The question was asked centuries ago, "Can you fathom the mysteries of God?" (Job 11:7). The answer is no! Unless God reveals himself, we are doomed to confusion and conjecture.

It is obvious that among those who believe in God there are many ideas abroad today as to what God is like. Some, for instance, believe God to be a celestial killjoy. They view him as peering over the balcony of heaven looking for anyone who seems to be enjoying life. On finding such a person, he shouts down, "Cut it out!"

Others think of God as a sentimental grandfather of the sky, rocking benignly and stroking his beard as he says, "Boys will be boys!" That everything will work out in the end, no matter what you have done, is conceded to be his general attitude toward people.

Others think of him as a big ball of fire and of us as little sparks who will eventually come back to the big ball. Still others, like Einstein, think of God as an impersonal force or mind. Herbert Spencer, one of the popularizers of agnosticism of a century ago, observed accurately that a bird has never been known to fly out of space. Therefore he concluded by analogy that it is impossible for the finite to penetrate the infinite. His observation was correct, but his conclusion was wrong. He missed one other possibility: that the infinite could penetrate the finite. This, of course, is what God did.

God Has Penetrated the Finite

As the writer to the Hebrews puts it, "In the past God spoke to our forefathers through the prophets at many times and in various ways, but in these last days he has spoken to us by his Son, whom he appointed heir of all things, and through whom he made the universe" (Heb 1:1-2).

God has taken the initiative, throughout history, to communicate to man. His fullest revelation has been his invasion into human history in the person of Jesus Christ. Here, in terms of human personality that we can understand, he has lived among us. If you wanted to communicate your love to a colony of ants, how could you most effectively do it? Clearly, it would be best to become an ant. Only in this way could your existence and what you were like be communicated fully and effectively. This is what God did with us. We are, as J. B. Phillips aptly put it, "the visited planet." The best and clearest answer to how we know there is a God is that he has visited us. The other indications are merely clues or hints. What confirms them conclusively is the birth, life, death and resurrection of Jesus Christ.

Changed Lives

Other evidence for the reality of God's existence is his clear presence in the lives of men and women today. Where Jesus Christ is believed and trusted, a profound change takes place in the individual, and ultimately, the community. One of the most moving illustrations of this is recorded by Ernest Gordon, who became chaplain at Princeton University. In his *Through the Valley of the Kwai,* he tells how, during World War II, the prisoners of the Japanese on the Malay peninsula had been reduced almost to animals, stealing food from their buddies who were also starving. In their desperation, the prisoners decided it would be good to read the New Testament.

Because Gordon was a university graduate, they asked him to lead. By his own admission he was a skeptic, and those who asked him to lead them were unbelievers too. He and others came to trust Christ on becoming acquainted with him in all of his beauty and power through the uncluttered simplicity of the New Testament. How this group of scrounging, clawing humans was transformed into a community of love is a touching and powerful story that demonstrates clearly the reality of God in Jesus Christ. Many others today, in less dramatic terms, have experienced this same reality.

There is, then, evidence from creation, history and contemporary life that there is a God and that this God can be known in personal experience.

For Individual or Group Study

1. What, according to the author, must occur for something to be scientifically proven (p. 23)?

2. Why can't the existence of God be proven in this way?

3. According to anthropology, all of the world's cultures originally believed in one God who was the creator. Why would atheists feel they had the upper hand if they could prove this were not so?

4. Summarize the evidence for God's existence based on the law of cause and effect and the fact of the universe's apparent order and design (pp. 25-32).

5. What do you think of the theory of "infinite time plus chance"? What would you say to someone who believed this theory?

6. What is the "moral argument" for the existence of God (pp. 32-33)?

7. How would you argue for or against the "moral argument"?

8. Paul Little offers the evidence of "changed lives" as further proof of God's existence (pp. 35-36). Because this evidence is subjective, it could be hardest to prove and easiest to counterfeit. Would the testimony of a born-again Christian sound very different from a person whose life was transformed by newfound faith in another religion? Why or why not?

9. If you were to give "changed lives" as an evidence of God's existence, what personal evidence would you be able to offer?

10. What other arguments for or against the existence of God can you think of?

11. Which of the arguments for God's existence seem most helpful to you in explaining the plausibility of God's existence? Why?

12. Which ones seem least helpful? Why?

13. If you would like to gain experience explaining the evidence for God's existence, think of someone who may be interested in hearing your reasons for believing. Consider setting up a time to talk to that person about your reasons for believing in God.

14. Take time now to add any new insights to your list of reasons for putting your hope in God through Christ Jesus. Space is provided following page 173.

For Further Reading

Evans, C. Stephen. *The Quest of Faith.* Downers Grove, Ill.: InterVarsity Press, 1986.

Lewis, C. S. *Mere Christianity.* New York: Macmillan, 1952; London: Collins, 1955.

3
Is Christ God?

●●●●●●●●●●

I T IS IMPOSSIBLE FOR US TO KNOW CONCLUSIVELY WHETHER GOD
exists and what he is like unless he takes the initiative and reveals
himself. In order to relate to God, we must know what he is like
and his attitude toward us. Suppose we knew he existed, but that
he was like Adolf Hitler—capricious, vicious, prejudiced and cruel.
What a horrible realization that would be!

We must scan the horizon of history to see if there is any clue
to God's revelation. There is one clear clue. In an obscure village
in Palestine, almost 2,000 years ago, a child was born in a stable.
His birth was feared by the reigning monarch, Herod. In an attempt
to destroy this baby, who was said to be the king of the Jews, Herod
had many infants killed in what history knows as the "slaughter
of the innocents" (Mt 2:1-18).

The baby and his parents settled in Nazareth, where Jesus

learned his father's trade of carpentry. He was an unusual child. When he was twelve years old, he confounded the scholars and rabbis in Jerusalem. When his parents remonstrated with him because he had stayed behind after they departed, he made the strange reply, "Didn't you know I had to be in my Father's house?" (Lk 2:49). This answer implied a unique relationship between him and God.

He lived in obscurity until he was thirty, and then he began a public ministry that lasted for three years. It was destined to change the course of history.

He was a kindly person and we're told that "the common people heard him gladly." And, "he taught as one who had authority, and not as their teachers of the law" (Mt 7:29).

Jesus Said He Was the Son of God

It soon became apparent, however, that he was making shocking and startling statements about himself. He began to identify himself as far more than a remarkable teacher or a prophet. He began to say clearly that he was deity. He made his identity the focal point of his teaching. The all-important question he put to those who followed him was, "Who do you say I am?" When Peter answered and said, "You are the Christ, the Son of the living God" (Mt 16:15-16), Jesus was not shocked, nor did he rebuke Peter. On the contrary, he commended him!

He made the claim explicitly, and his hearers got the full impact of his words. We are told, "The Jews tried all the harder to kill him; not only was he breaking the Sabbath, but he was even calling God his own Father, making himself equal with God" (Jn 5:18).

On another occasion he said, "I and the Father are one" (Jn 10:30). Immediately the Jews wanted to stone him. He asked them for which good work they wanted to kill him. They replied, "We are not stoning you for any of these, . . . but for blasphemy, because you, a mere man, claim to be God" (10:33).

Jesus clearly claimed attributes which only God has. When a paralytic was let down through a roof and placed at his feet, he said, "Son, your sins are forgiven" (Mk 2:5). This caused a great to-do among the scribes, who said in their hearts, "Why does this fellow talk like that? He's blaspheming! Who can forgive sins but God alone?" (2:7).

Jesus, knowing their thoughts, said to them, "Which is easier: to say to the paralytic, 'Your sins are forgiven,' or to say, 'Get up, take your mat and walk'?" (2:9). (Then he said, in effect, "But that you may know that I, the Son of Man, have authority on earth to forgive sins [which you rightly say God alone can do, but which is invisible], I'll do something you can see.") Turning to the palsied man, he commanded him, "I tell you, get up, take your mat and go home" (2:11).

That the title *Son of Man* is an assertion of deity, rather than being a disclaimer of it as some have suggested, is seen in the attributes Jesus claims as Son of Man. These obviously are true only of God.

At the critical moment when his life was at stake because of this claim, he asserted it to the high priest, who had put the question to him directly. "The high priest asked him, 'Are you the Christ, the Son of the Blessed One?' 'I am,' said Jesus. 'And you will see the Son of Man sitting at the right hand of the Mighty One and coming on the clouds of heaven.' The high priest tore his clothes. 'Why do we need any more witnesses?' he asked. 'You have heard the blasphemy' " (Mk 14:61-64).

John Stott sums it up, "So close was his connection with God that he equated a man's attitude to himself with the man's attitude to God. Thus, to know him was to know God (Jn 8:19; 14:7). To see him was to see God (12:45; 14:9). To believe in him was to believe in God (12:44; 14:1). To receive him was to receive God (Mk 9:37). To hate him was to hate God (Jn 15:23). And to honor him was to honor God (5:23)."[1]

Only Four Possibilities

As we face the claims of Christ, there are only four possibilities. He was either a liar, a lunatic, a legend or the Truth. If we say he is not the Truth, we are automatically affirming one of the other three alternatives, whether we realize it or not. When friends of ours take this position, we should invite them to show us what evidence they have that would lead us to adopt it. Often they realize, for the first time, that there is no evidence to support their views. Rather, all the evidence points in the other direction.

■ *One possibility is that Jesus Christ lied when he said he was God*—that he knew he was not God but deliberately deceived his hearers to lend authority to his teaching. Few, if any, seriously hold this position. Even those who deny his deity affirm that they think Jesus was a great moral teacher. They fail to realize those two statements are a contradiction. Jesus could hardly be a great moral teacher if, on the most crucial point of his teaching—his identity—he was a deliberate liar.

■ *A kinder, though no less shocking possibility, is that he was sincere but self-deceived.* We have a name for a person today who thinks he is God—or a poached egg! That name is lunatic, and it certainly would apply to Christ if he were deceived on this all-important issue.

But as we look at the life of Christ, we see no evidence of the abnormality and imbalance we find in a deranged person. Rather, we find the greatest composure under pressure. At his trial before Pilate, when his very life was at stake, he was calm and serene. As C. S. Lewis put it, "The discrepancy between the depth and sanity of his moral teaching and the rampant megalomania which must lie behind his theological teaching unless he is indeed God has never been satisfactorily got over."[2]

■ *The third alternative is that all of the talk about his claiming to be God is a legend*—that what actually happened was that his enthusiastic followers, in the third and fourth centuries, put words into his mouth he would have been shocked to hear. Were he to return he would immediately repudiate them.

The legend theory has been significantly refuted by many discoveries of modern archaeology. These have conclusively shown that the four biographies of Christ were written within the lifetime of contemporaries of Christ. Some time ago Dr. William F. Albright, world-famous archaeologist now retired from Johns Hopkins University, said that there was no reason to believe that any of the Gospels were written later than A.D. 70. For a mere legend about Christ, in the form of the gospel, to have gained the circulation and to have had the impact it had, without one shred of basis in fact, is incredible.

For this to have happened would be as fantastic as for someone in our own time to write a biography of the late Franklin Delano Roosevelt and in it say he claimed to be God, to forgive people's sins and to have risen from the dead. Such a story is so wild it would never get off the ground because there are still too many people around who knew Roosevelt! The legend theory does not hold water in the light of the early date of the Gospel manuscripts.

■ *The only other alternative is that Jesus spoke the truth.*

From one point of view, however, claims don't mean much. Talk is cheap. Anyone can make claims. There have been others who have claimed deity. A recent one was Father Divine of Philadelphia, now deceased. I could claim to be God, and you could claim to be God, but the question all of us must answer is, "What credentials do we bring to substantiate our claim?" In my case it wouldn't take you five minutes to disprove my claim. It probably wouldn't take too much more to dispose of yours. It certainly wasn't difficult to show that Father Divine was not God. But when it comes to Jesus of Nazareth, it's not so simple. He had the credentials to back up his claim. He said, "Even though you do not believe me, believe the miracles, that you may know and understand that the Father is in me, and I in the Father" (Jn 10:38).

What Were Jesus' Credentials?

■ *First, his moral character coincided with his claims.*

We saw earlier that many asylum inmates claim to be celebrities or deities but their claims are belied by their characters. Not so with Christ. And we do not compare Christ with others; we contrast him with all others. He is unique—as unique as God.

Jesus Christ was sinless. The caliber of his life was such that he was able to challenge his enemies with the question, "Can any of you prove me guilty of sin?" (Jn 8:46). He was met by silence, even though he addressed those who would have liked to point out a flaw in his character.

We read of the temptations of Jesus, but we never hear of a confession of sin on his part. He never asked for forgiveness, though he told his followers to do so.

This lack of any sense of moral failure on Jesus' part is astonishing in view of the fact that it is completely contrary to the experience of the saints and mystics in all ages. The closer men and women draw to God, the more overwhelmed they are with their own failure, corruption and shortcoming. The closer one is to a shining light, the more he realizes his need of a bath. This is true also, in the moral realm, for ordinary mortals.

It is also striking that John, Paul and Peter, all of whom were trained from earliest childhood to believe in the universality of sin, all spoke of the sinlessness of Christ: "He committed no sin, and no deceit was found in his mouth" (1 Pet 2:22); "In him is no sin" (1 Jn 3:5); Jesus "had no sin" (2 Cor 5:21).

Pilate, no friend of Jesus, said, "I find no basis for a charge against him" (Jn 18:38). He implicitly recognized Christ's innocence. And the Roman centurion who witnessed the death of Christ said "Surely he was the Son of God!" (Mt 27:54).

In Jesus we find the perfect personality. Bernard Ramm points out:

If God were a man, we would expect his personality to be true humanity. Only God could tell us what a true man should be like. Certainly there are anticipations of the perfect man in the piety of the Old Testament. Foremost must be a complete God-consciousness, coupled with a complete dedication and consecration of life to God. Then, ranked below this, are the other virtues, graces and attributes that characterize perfect humanity. Intelligence must not stifle piety, and prayer must not be a substitute for work, and zeal must not be irrational fanaticism, and reserve must not become stolidity. In Christ we have the perfect blend of personality traits, because as God Incarnate he is perfect humanity. Schaff describes our Lord, with reference to this point of our discussion, as follows: "His zeal never degenerated into passion, nor his constancy into obstinacy, nor his benevolence into weakness, nor his tenderness into sentimentality. His unworldliness was free from indifference and unsociability or undue familiarity; his self-denial from moroseness; his temperance from austerity. He combined childlike innocency with manly strength, absorbing devotion to God with untiring interest in the welfare of man, tender love to the sinner with uncompromising severity against sin, commanding dignity with winning humility, fearless courage with wise caution, unyielding firmness with sweet gentleness!"[3]

■ *Christ demonstrated a power over natural forces which could belong only to God, the author of these forces.*

He stilled a raging storm of wind and waves on the Sea of Galilee. In doing this he provoked from those in the boat the awestruck question, "Who is this? Even the wind and the waves obey him!" (Mk 4:41). He turned water into wine and fed 5,000 people from five loaves and two fish, gave a grieving widow back her only son by raising him from the dead and brought to life the dead daughter of a shattered father. To an old friend he said, "Lazarus, come forth!" and dramatically raised him from the dead. It is most significant that his enemies did not deny this miracle.

Rather, they tried to kill him. "If we let him go on like this," they said, "everyone will believe in him" (Jn 11:48).

■ *Jesus demonstrated the Creator's power over sickness and disease.*

He made the lame to walk, the dumb to speak and the blind to see. Some of his healings were congenital problems not susceptible to psychosomatic cure. The most outstanding was that of the blind man whose case is recorded in John 9. Though the man couldn't answer his speculative questioners, his experience was enough to convince *him.* "One thing I do know. I was blind but now I see!" he declared (Jn 9:25). He was astounded that his friends didn't recognize his healer as the Son of God. "Nobody has ever heard of opening the eyes of a man born blind," he said (9:32). To him the evidence was obvious.

■ *Jesus' supreme credential to authenticate his claim to deity was his resurrection from the dead.*

Five times in the course of his life he predicted he would die. He also predicted how he would die and that three days later he would rise from the dead and appear to his disciples. Surely this was the great test. It was a claim that was easy to verify. It either happened or it didn't.

The resurrection is so crucial and foundational a subject we will devote a whole chapter to it. If the resurrection happened, there is no difficulty with any other miracles. And if we establish the resurrection, we have the answer to the big question of God, his character and our relationship to him. An answer to this question makes it possible to answer all subsidiary questions.

Christ moved history as only God could do. Schaff very graphically says:

> This Jesus of Nazareth without money and arms, conquered more millions than Alexander, Caesar, Muhammad and Napoleon; without science and learning, he shed more light on matters human and divine than all philosophers and scholars com-

bined; without the eloquence of schools, he spoke such words of life as were never spoken before or since and produced effects which lie beyond the reach of orator or poet; without writing a single line, he set more pens in motion and furnished themes for more sermons, orations, discussions, learned volumes, works of art and songs of praise than the whole army of great men of ancient and modern times.

■ *Finally, we know that Christ is God because we can experience him in the twentieth century.*

Experience in itself is not conclusive, but combined with the historic objective of the resurrection it gives us the basis for our solid conviction. There is no other hypothesis to explain all the data we have than the profound fact that Jesus Christ is God the Son.

For Individual or Group Study

1. In what ways did Jesus Christ claim to be the Son of God (pp. 40-44)?

2. When we face the claims of Christ, there are four possible ways to explain his actions: he was a liar, a lunatic, a legend or the Son of God (pp. 42-43). What evidence exists to disprove that Jesus was a liar?

3. What evidence exists for or against the theory that Jesus was a lunatic?

4. Why might it be argued that the Gospels are accounts of an actual person, not a legend?

5. Many people claim that Jesus was a "great moral teacher" but not the Son of God. How would you answer such a person?

6. How did Jesus substantiate his claim to being God's Son (pp. 44-46)?

7. Reread the description of Jesus written by Bernard Ramm (pp. 44-45). What aspect of his character would you find most comforting to have in a best friend?

8. What aspect you would like to emulate most? How can you begin to develop this more?

9. Take time now to add any new insights to your list of reasons for putting your hope in God through Christ Jesus. Space is provided following page 173.

For Further Reading

Bruce, F. F. *Jesus: Lord and Savior.* Downers Grove, Ill.: InterVarsity Press; London: Hodder and Stoughton, 1986.

Green, Michael, ed. *The Truth of God Incarnate.* London: Hodder and Stoughton, 1977.

Kreeft, Peter. *Between Heaven and Hell.* Downers Grove, Ill.: InterVarsity Press, 1982.

Stott, John R. W. *The Authentic Jesus.* Downers Grove, Ill.: InterVarsity Press, 1986.

4
Did Christ Rise from the Dead?

● ● ● ● ● ● ● ● ● ● ●

BOTH FRIENDS AND ENEMIES OF THE CHRISTIAN FAITH HAVE recognized the resurrection of Christ to be the foundation stone of the faith. Paul, the great apostle, wrote to those in Corinth, who in general denied the resurrection of the dead: "If Christ has not been raised, our preaching is useless and so is your faith" (1 Cor 15:14). Paul rested his whole case on the bodily resurrection of Christ. Either he did or he didn't rise from the dead. If he did, it was the most sensational event in all of history, and we have conclusive answers to the profound questions of our existence: Where have we come from? Why are we here? Where are we going? If Christ rose, we know with certainty that God exists, what he is like and how we may know him in personal experience; the universe takes on meaning and purpose, and it is possible to experience the living God in contemporary life. These and many other wonderful things are true if Jesus of Nazareth rose from the dead.

Not Wishful Thinking

On the other hand, if Christ did not rise from the dead, Christianity is an interesting museum piece—nothing more. It has no objective validity or reality. Though it is a nice wishful thought, it certainly isn't worth getting steamed up about. The martyrs who went singing to the lions, and contemporary missionaries who have given their lives in Ecuador and Congo while taking this message to others, have been poor deluded fools.

The attack on Christianity by its enemies has most often concentrated on the resurrection because it has been correctly seen that this event is the crux of the matter. A remarkable attack was the one contemplated in the early 1930s by a young British lawyer. He was convinced that the resurrection was a mere tissue of fable and fantasy. Sensing that it was the foundation stone of the Christian faith, he decided to do the world a favor by once and for all exposing this fraud and superstition. As a lawyer, he felt he had the critical faculties to rigidly sift evidence and to admit nothing as evidence which did not meet the stiff criteria for admission into a law court today.

However, while Frank Morison was doing his research, a remarkable thing happened. The case was not nearly as easy as he had supposed. As a result the first chapter in his book *Who Moved the Stone?* is entitled, "The Book That Refused to Be Written." In it he described how, as he examined the evidence, he became persuaded against his will of the fact of the bodily resurrection.

Data to Be Considered

What are some of the pieces of data to be considered in answering the question, "Did Christ rise from the dead?"

■ *First, there is the fact of the Christian church.* It is worldwide in scope. Its history can be traced back to Palestine around A.D.

32. Did it just happen or was there a cause for it? These people who were first called Christians at Antioch turned the world of their time upside-down. They constantly referred to the resurrection as the basis for their teaching, preaching, living and—significantly—dying.

■ *Then there is the fact of the Christian day.* Sunday is the day of worship for Christians. Its history can also be traced back to the year A.D. 32. Such a shift in the calendar was monumental, and something cataclysmic must have happened to change the day of worship from the Jewish sabbath, the seventh day of the week, to Sunday, the first day. Christians said the shift came because of their desire to celebrate the resurrection of Jesus from the dead. This shift is all the more remarkable when we remember that the first Christians were Jews. If the resurrection does not account for this change, what does?

■ *Third, there is the Christian book, the New Testament.* In its pages are contained six independent testimonies to the fact of the resurrection. Three of them are by eyewitnesses: John, Peter and Matthew. Paul, writing to the churches at an early date, referred to the resurrection in such a way that it is obvious that to him and his readers the event was well known and accepted without question. Are these men, who helped transform the moral structure of society, consummate liars or deluded madmen? These alternatives are harder to believe than the fact of the resurrection, and there is no shred of evidence to support them.

Two facts must be explained by the believer and the unbeliever alike. They are the empty tomb and the alleged appearances of Jesus Christ.

Accounting for the Empty Tomb

■ *The earliest explanation circulated was that the disciples stole the body!* In Matthew 28:11-15, we have the record of the reaction of the chief priests and the elders when the guards gave them the infuriating and mysterious news that the body was gone. They gave the soldiers money and told them to explain that the disciples had come at night and stolen the body while they were asleep. That story was so obviously false that Matthew didn't even bother to refute it! What judge would listen to you if you said that while you were asleep your neighbor came into your house and stole your television set? Who knows what goes on while he's asleep? Testimony like this would be laughed out of any court.

Furthermore, we are faced with a psychological and ethical impossibility. Stealing the body of Christ is something totally foreign to the character of the disciples and all that we know of them. It would mean that they were perpetrators of a deliberate lie which was responsible for the deception and ultimate death of thousands of people. It is inconceivable that even if a few of the disciples had conspired and pulled off this theft they would never have told the others.

Each of the disciples faced the test of torture and martyrdom for his statements and beliefs. People will die for what they *believe* to be true, though it may actually be false. They do not, however, die for what they know is a lie. If ever a person tells the truth, it is on his or her deathbed. And if the disciples had taken the body, and Christ were still dead, we would still have the problem of explaining his alleged appearances.

■ *A second hypothesis is that the authorities, Jewish or Roman, moved the body!* But why? Having put guards at the tomb, what would be their reason for moving the body? But there is also a convincing answer for this thesis—the silence of the authorities in the face of the apostles' bold preaching in Jerusalem about the resurrection. The ecclesiastical leaders were seething with rage and did everything possible to prevent the spread of this message and to suppress it (Acts 4). They arrested Peter and John and beat and threatened them in an attempt to close their mouths.

But there was a very simple solution to their problem. If they had Christ's body, they could have paraded it through the streets of Jerusalem. In one fell swoop they would have successfully smothered Christianity in its cradle. That they did not do this bears eloquent testimony to the fact that they did not have the body.

■ *Another popular theory has been that the women, distraught and overcome by grief, missed their way in the dimness of the morning and went to the wrong tomb.* In their distress they *imagined* Christ had risen because the tomb was empty. This theory, however, falls before the same fact that destroys the previous one. If the women went to the wrong tomb, why did the high priests and other enemies of the faith not go to the right tomb and produce the body? Further, it is inconceivable that all Jesus' followers would succumb to the same mistake, and certainly Joseph of Arimathea, owner of the tomb, would have solved the problem. In addition, it must be remembered that this was a private burial ground, not a public cemetery. There was no other tomb nearby that would have allowed them to make this mistake.

■ *The swoon theory has also been advanced to explain the empty tomb.* In this view, Christ did not actually die. He was mistakenly reported to be dead but had swooned from exhaustion, pain and loss of blood. When he was laid in the coolness of the tomb, he revived. He came out of the tomb and appeared to his disciples, who mistakenly thought he had risen from the dead.

This is a theory of modern construction. It first appeared at the end of the eighteenth century. It is significant that not a suggestion of this kind has come down from antiquity among all the violent attacks which have been made on Christianity. All of the earliest records are emphatic about Jesus' death.

But let us assume for a moment that Christ was buried alive and swooned. Is it possible to believe that he would have survived three days in a damp tomb without food or water or attention of any kind? Would he have survived being wound in spice-laden graveclothes? Would he have had the strength to extricate himself from the graveclothes, push the heavy stone away from the mouth of the grave, overcome the Roman guards and walk miles on feet that had been pierced with spikes? Such a belief is more fantastic than the simple fact of the resurrection itself.

Even the German critic David Strauss, who by no means believes in the resurrection, rejected this idea as incredible. He said:

It is impossible that One who had just come forth from the grave half dead, who crept about weak and ill, who stood in the need of medical treatment, of bandaging, strengthening, and tender care, and who at last succumbed to suffering, could ever have given the disciples the impression that he was a conqueror over death and the grave; that he was the Prince of Life. This lay at the bottom of their future ministry. Such a resuscitation could only have weakened the impression which he had made upon them in life and in death—or at the most, could have given in an elegiac voice—but could by no possibility have changed their sorrow into enthusiasm or elevated their reverence into worship.[1]

Finally, if this theory is correct, Christ himself was involved in flagrant lies. His disciples believed and preached that he was dead but came alive again. Jesus did nothing to dispel this belief, but rather encouraged it. The only theory that adequately explains the empty tomb is the resurrection of Jesus Christ from the dead.

The Appearances of Christ

The second piece of data that everyone, whether believer or unbeliever, must explain is the recorded appearances of Christ. These occurred from the morning of his resurrection to his ascension forty days later. Ten distinct appearances are recorded. They show great variety as to time, place and people. Two were to individuals, Peter and James. There were appearances to the disciples as a group, and one was to 500 assembled brethren. The appearances were at different places. Some were in the garden near his tomb, some were in the Upper Room. One was on the road from Jerusalem to Emmaus, and some were far away in Galilee. Each appearance was characterized by different acts and words by Jesus.

For the same reasons that the empty tomb cannot be explained on the basis of lies or legends, neither can we dismiss the statement of the appearances of Christ on this basis. This is testimony given by eyewitnesses—fully and profoundly convinced of the truth of their statements.

The major theory advanced to explain away the accounts of the appearances of Christ is that they were hallucinations. At first, this sounds like a plausible explanation of an otherwise supernatural event. It is plausible until we begin to realize that modern medicine has observed that certain laws apply to such psychological phenomena. As we relate these principles to the evidence at hand, we see that what at first seemed most plausible is, in fact, impossible.

Hallucinations occur generally in people who tend to be vividly imaginative and of a nervous make-up. But the appearances of Christ were to all sorts of people. True, some were sensitive, but there were also hardheaded fishermen like Peter and others of various dispositions.

Hallucinations are extremely subjective and individual. For this reason, no two people have the same experience. But in the case of the resurrection, Christ appeared not just to individuals but to groups, including one of more than 500 people. Paul said that more than half of them were still alive and could tell about these events (1 Cor 15).

Hallucinations usually occur only at particular times and places, and are associated with the events fancied. But these appearances occurred both indoors and outdoors, in the morning, afternoon and evening.

Generally, these psychic experiences occur over a long period of time with some regularity. But these experiences happened during a period of forty days, and then stopped abruptly. No one ever said they happened again.

But perhaps the most conclusive indication of the fallacy of the hallucination theory is a fact often overlooked. In order to have an experience like this, one must so intensely want to believe that he or she projects something that really isn't there and attaches reality to his imagination. For instance, a mother who has lost a son in the war remembers how he used to come home from work every evening at 5:30. She sits in her rocking chair every afternoon, musing and meditating. Finally, she thinks she sees him come through the door and has a conversation with him. At this point she has lost contact with reality.

One might think that this is what happened to the disciples about the resurrection. The fact is that the opposite took place—they were persuaded against their wills that Jesus had risen from the dead!

Mary came to the tomb on the first Easter Sunday morning with spices in her hands. Why? To anoint the dead body of the Lord she loved. She was obviously not expecting to find him risen from the dead. In fact, when she first saw him she mistook him for the gardener! It was only after he spoke to her and identified himself that she realized who he was.

When the other disciples heard, they didn't believe. The story seemed to them "as an idle tale."

When the Lord finally appeared to the disciples, they were frightened and thought they were seeing a ghost! They thought they were having a hallucination, and it jolted them. He finally had to tell them, "Touch me and see; a ghost does not have flesh and bones, as you see I have." He asked them if they had any food, and they gave him a piece of broiled fish. Luke didn't add the obvious—ghosts don't eat fish! (Lk 24:36-43).

Finally, there is the classic case of which we still speak—Thomas the doubter. He was not present when the Lord appeared to the disciples the first time. They told him about it, but he scoffed and would not believe. In effect, he said, "I'm from Missouri. I won't believe unless I'm shown. I'm an empiricist. Unless I can put my finger into the nail wounds in his hands and my hand into his side, I will not believe." *He* wasn't about to have a hallucination!

John gives us the graphic story (Jn 20) of our Lord's appearance to the disciples eight days later. He graciously invited Thomas to examine the evidence of his hands and his side. Thomas looked at him and fell down in worship: "My Lord and my God."

To hold the hallucination theory in explaining the appearances of Christ, one must completely ignore the evidence.

What was it that changed a band of frightened, cowardly disciples into men of courage and conviction? What was it that changed Peter from one who, the night before the crucifixion, was so afraid for his own skin that he three times denied he even knew Jesus, into a roaring lion of the faith? Some fifty days later Peter risked his life by saying he had seen Jesus risen from the dead. It must be remembered that Peter preached his electric Pentecost sermon in Jerusalem, where the events took place and his life was in danger. He was not in Galilee, miles away where no one could verify the facts and where his ringing statements might go unchallenged.

Only the bodily resurrection of Christ could have produced this change.

Contemporary Proof

Finally, there is the evidence for the resurrection which is contemporary and personal. If Jesus Christ rose from the dead, he is alive today, ready to invade and change those who invite him into their lives. Thousands now living bear uniform testimony that their lives have been revolutionized by Jesus Christ. He has done in them what he said he would do. The proof of the pudding is in the eating. The invitation still stands, "Taste and see that the LORD is good!" (Ps 34:8). The avenue of experimentation is open to each person.

In summary, then, we can agree with Canon Westcott, a brilliant scholar at Cambridge, who said, "Indeed, taking all the evidence together, it is not too much to say that there is no historic incident better or more variously supported than the resurrection of Christ. Nothing but the antecedent assumption that it must be false could have suggested the idea of deficiency in the proof of it."[2]

For Individual or Group Study

1. Read 1 Corinthians 15:3-28. The apostle Paul says in these verses that the resurrection of Jesus Christ is "of first importance" (v. 3) for proof of Christ's deity, the reversal of Adam's sin that resulted in death and assurance of our eternal life. How did Christ's resurrection accomplish these things?

2. Paul Little points out how the Christian church, the Christian sabbath and the Christian Scriptures were changed by Jesus' resurrection (pp. 50-51). How would your life be different if Jesus had never risen from the dead?

3. Read Matthew 28:11-15. Even Jesus' enemies admitted that his tomb was empty. The truth of Christ's resurrection rests on *how* the tomb was emptied. The authorities claimed that Jesus' followers removed the body. Given all that the disciples later endured to spread the word of Christ's resurrection, how likely does the author think this is (pp. 51-52)?

4. Other explanations often given are that the authorities moved the body or the disciples returned to the wrong tomb (pp. 52-53). What makes these answers reasonable or unreasonable?

5. A more recent explanation suggests Jesus never really died but instead merely fainted (pp. 53-54). What makes this theory plausible?

What "loose ends" would this theory leave?

6. At the time the New Testaments books were written, there were still many alive who claimed to have seen Jesus alive again after his execution. Three explanations are that the people lied, hallucinated or indeed saw him (pp. 54-57). What evidence confirms or denies each of these?

7. Some of the greatest proofs of Jesus' resurrection are (1) the difficulty Jesus had in convincing his followers he was again alive; and (2) how the news changed them from fearful fugitives to bold, aggressive witnesses. How has your life been changed by belief in the resurrection?

8. Is there some way you would like to act on your belief in Christ's claims and power?

9. Take time now to add any new insights to your list of reasons for putting your hope in God through Christ Jesus. Space is provided following page 173.

For Further Reading

Anderson, J. N. D. *Evidence for the Resurrection*. Downers Grove, Ill.: InterVarsity Press, 1966.

Crossley, Robert S. *The Trinity*. Downers Grove, Ill.: InterVarsity Press, 1987.

Green, Michael. *The Day Death Died*. Downers Grove, Ill.: InterVarsity Press, 1982.

——————. *The Empty Cross of Christ*. Downers Grove, Ill.:InterVarsity Press, 1984.

Morison, Frank. *Who Moved the Stone?* Downers Grove, Ill.: InterVarsity Press, 1958.

5
Is the Bible God's Word?

● ● ● ● ● ● ● ● ● ●

'All scripture is given by inspiration of God, and profitable...

I HEARD ABOUT A CHRISTIAN FAMILY THAT PRAYED OUT LOUD TO-gether several times each day. One day the youngest son looked up at a picture of Jesus on the kitchen wall, stared at it and said thoughtfully, "Jesus, Jesus, Jesus. That's all I hear. But he don't say nothin' back!"

Fortunately for us, Jesus does say something back. A lot! Peter tells us he has communicated to us all we need to know "for life and godliness." But the question continues to arise: Is the Bible in its totality the Word of God?

As important as this question is, it is not the starting point in explaining the Christian faith to a non-Christian. It's easy to get bogged down in trying to prove the inspiration of the Bible and never get to the crucial issue in salvation, which is one's relation-ship with Jesus Christ. The Bible *is* the Word of God regardless of what a person may think about it. A non-Christian can be led to consider the message and content of Scripture even before coming to the question of divine inspiration. The crucial question is, "What do you think of Jesus Christ?" rather than "What is your view of the Bible?"

All we need do to confront a person with the claims of Jesus Christ is to show him that the Gospels are reliable historical documents. This is reasonably easy, as we shall see in a later chapter. After a person has trusted Christ, the logical question for him or her to ask is, "How did Jesus Christ view the Bible?" As we shall see, it is abundantly clear he viewed Scripture as the authoritative Word of God. Then as a follower of Christ, the logical step of obedience is to accept his view of Scripture.

But how can we answer this far-reaching question for ourselves as believers? While the statements and claims of the Scriptures themselves are not proof, they are a significant body of data which cannot be ignored.

Beethoven Was Not "God-Breathed"

The Bible describes itself as "given by inspiration of God and . . . profitable for doctrine, for reproof, for correction, for instruction in righteousness" (2 Tim 3:16 KJV). The word *inspired,* here, is not to be confused with the common usage of the word, as when we say Shakespeare was inspired to write great plays, or Beethoven was inspired to compose great symphonies. Inspiration, in the biblical sense, is unique. The word translated "inspired" actually means *God-breathed* as it has been translated in the New International Version. It refers, not to the writers, but to the words that have been written. This is an important point to grasp.

"That which is breathed out by God" clearly tells us where the Bible originated. Old Testament "prophecy never had its origin in the will of man, but men spoke from God as they were carried along by the Holy Spirit" (2 Pet 1:21). The Bible is the product of God himself. These are not mere human ideas, but God's divine character and will is revealed through these words.

It is important to realize too that the writers of the Scripture were not mere writing machines. God did not punch them, like keys on a typewriter, to produce his message. He did not dictate the words, as the biblical view of inspiration has so often been caricatured. It is quite clear that each writer has a style of his own. Jeremiah does not write like Isaiah, and John does not write like Paul. God worked through the instrumentality of human personality, but so guided and controlled people that what they wrote is *what he wanted written.*

Other indications of the claim of supernatural origin of Scripture are sprinkled throughout its contents. Prophets were consciously God's mouthpieces and spoke as such: "The word of the Lord came to me" is a phrase that recurs frequently in the Old Testament. David says, "The Spirit of the LORD spoke through me; his word was on my tongue" (2 Sam 23:2). Jeremiah said, "The LORD reached out his hand and touched my mouth and said to me, 'Now, I have put my words in your mouth' " (Jer 1:9).

It is also very remarkable that when later writers of Scripture quote parts of the Scripture which had previously been recorded, they frequently quote it as words spoken by God rather than by a particular prophet. For instance, Paul writes, "The Scripture foresaw that God would justify the Gentiles by faith, and announced the gospel in advance to Abraham: 'All nations will be blessed through you' " (Gal 3:8).

There are other passages in which God is spoken of as if he were the Scriptures. For example, "Sovereign Lord, . . . you spoke by the Holy Spirit through the mouth of your servant, our father David: 'Why do the nations rage and the peoples plot in vain?' " (Acts 4:24-25 quoting Ps 2:1). Benjamin Warfield points out that these instances of the Scriptures being spoken of as if they were God, and of God being spoken of as if he were the Scriptures, could only result from a habitual identification, in the mind of the writer, of the text of Scripture with God speaking. It became natural, then, to use the phrase "Scripture said" and to use the phrase "God says" when what was really intended was, "Scripture, the Word of God, says. . . ." The two sets of passages, together, thus show an absolute identification of *Scripture* with the speaking God.[1]

It is equally clear that New Testament writers have the same prophetic claim to authority as Old Testament writers. Jesus said that John the Baptist was a prophet and more than a prophet (Mt 11:9-15). As Gordon Clark has put it, "he was superior to all the Old Testament prophets. Yet the prophet who was least in New Testament times was a greater prophet than John. It follows, does it not, that the New Testament prophets were no less inspired than their forerunners?"[2]

Paul claims prophetic authority: "If anybody thinks he is a prophet or spiritually gifted, let him acknowledge that what I am writing to you is the Lord's command" (1 Cor 14:37).

Peter speaks of Paul's letters as that "which ignorant and unstable people distort, as they do the other Scriptures, to their own destruction" (2 Pet 3:16). His reference to them on the same level as "the other Scriptures" shows that he viewed them as having the prophetic authority of Scripture.

Jesus' View of Scripture

Most significant of all, however, is our Lord's view of the Scripture. What did he think of it? How did he use it? If we can answer these questions, we have the answer of the incarnate Word of God himself. Surely he is the authority for anyone who claims him as Lord!

What was our Lord's attitude toward the Old Testament? He states emphatically, "I tell you the truth, until heaven and earth disappear, not the smallest letter, not the least stroke of a pen, will by any means disappear from the Law until everything is accomplished" (Mt 5:18). He quoted Scripture as final authority, often introducing the statement with the phrase, "It is written," as in his encounter with Satan in the temptation in the wilderness (Mt 4). He spoke of himself and of events surrounding his life as being fulfillments of the Scripture (Mt 26:54, 56).

Perhaps his most sweeping endorsement and acceptance of the Old Testament was when he declared with finality, "The Scripture cannot be broken" (Jn 10:35).

If, then, we accept Jesus as Savior and Lord, it would be a contradiction in terms, and strangely inconsistent, if we rejected the Scripture as the Word of God. On this point we would be in disagreement with the one whom we acknowledge to be the eternal God, the Creator of the universe.

Some have suggested that in his view of the Old Testament, our Lord accommodated himself to the prejudices of his contemporary hearers. They accepted it as authoritative, so he appealed to it to gain wider acceptance for his teaching, though he himself did not subscribe to the popular view.

Grave difficulties beset this thesis, however. Our Lord's recognition and use of the authority of the Old Testament was not superficial and unessential. It was at the heart of his teaching concerning his person and work. He would be guilty of grave deception, and much of what he taught would be based on a fallacy. Then too why would he accommodate himself at this one point, when on other seemingly less important points he abrasively failed to accommodate himself to the prejudices of the time? This is most clearly illustrated in his attitude toward the sabbath. And we could ask an even more basic question: How do we know, if accommodation is his principle of operation, when he is accommodating himself to ignorance and prejudice and when he is not?

Helpful Definitions

Several definitions will be of great help in our understanding the Bible as the Word of God.

■ *Those who accept the Bible as the Word of God are often ac-*

cused of taking the Bible literally.

The question, "Do you believe the Bible literally?" is like the question, "Have you stopped beating your wife?" Either a yes or a no convicts the one who responds. Whenever the question is asked, the term literally must be carefully defined. Taking a literal view of the Bible does not mean we can't recognize that figures of speech are used in the Scripture. When Isaiah said "the trees of the field will clap their hands" (Is 55:12), and the psalmist said "mountains skipped like rams" (Ps 114:4, 6), it is not to be thought that one who takes the Bible literally views such statements as literal. No, there is poetry as well as prose and other literary forms in the Bible. We believe that the Bible is to be interpreted in the sense in which the authors intended it to be received by readers. This is the same principle one employs when reading the newspaper. And it is remarkably easy to distinguish between figures of speech and those statements a writer intends his readers to take literally.

This view is in contrast with that of those who do not take the Bible *literally*. They frequently attempt to evade the clear intent of the words, suggesting that the biblical records of certain events (for instance, the Fall of man, and miracles) are merely nonfactual stories to illustrate and convey profound spiritual truth.

Those holding this view say that as the truth of "Don't kill the goose that lays the golden egg" does not hinge on the literal factuality of Aesop's fable, so we need not insist on the historicity of biblical events and records to enjoy and realize the truth they convey. Some modern writers have applied this principle even to the cross and the resurrection of Jesus Christ. The expression "taking the Bible literally," therefore, is ambiguous and must be carefully defined to avoid great confusion.

■ *Another very important term we must clearly define is inerrancy.*

What does *inerrancy* mean and what does it not mean? Considerable confusion can be avoided by clear definition at this point. A temptation we must avoid is that of imposing on the biblical writers our twentieth-century standards of scientific and historical precision and accuracy. For instance, the Scripture describes things phenomenologically—that is, as they appear to be. It speaks of the sun rising and setting. Now, we know that the sun does not actually rise and set but that the earth rotates. But we use *sunrise* and *sunset* ourselves, even in an age of scientific enlightenment, because this is a convenient way of describing what appears to be. So we cannot charge the Bible with error when it speaks phenomenologically. Because it speaks in this way, it has been clear to people of all ages and cultures.

In ancient times there were not the same standards of exactness in historical matters. Sometimes round numbers are used rather than precise figures. When the police estimate a crowd we know the figure is not accurate, but it is close enough for their purpose.

Some apparent errors may be errors in transcription, which means that careful work is necessary in establishing the true text. We will discuss this more fully in the chapter on whether or not we can trust the Bible documents.

There are some other problems which as yet do not yield a ready explanation. We must freely admit this, remembering that many times in the past, problems resolved themselves when more data became available. The logical position, then, would seem to be that where there are areas of apparent conflict, we must hold the problem in abeyance, admitting our present inability to explain, but awaiting the possibility of new data. The presence of problems does not prevent our accepting the Bible as the supernatural Word of God.

E. J. Carnell puts it succinctly:

There is a close parallel between science and Christianity which surprisingly few seem to notice. As Christianity assumes that all in the Bible is supernatural, so the scientist assumes that all in nature is rational and orderly. Both are hypotheses—based, not on all of the evidence, but on the evidence "for the most part." Science devoutly holds to the hypothesis that all of nature is mechanical, though as a matter of fact the mysterious electron keeps jumping around as expressed by the Heisenberg principle of uncertainty. And how does science justify its hypothesis that all of nature is mechanical, when it admits on other grounds that many areas of nature do not seem to conform to this pattern? The answer is that since regularity is observed in nature "for the most part," the smoothest hypothesis is to assume that it is the same throughout the whole.[3]

■ *A further indication that the Bible is the Word of God is in the remarkable number of fulfilled prophecies it contains.*

These prophecies are not vague generalities like those given by modern fortunetellers: "A handsome man will soon come into your life." Such predictions are susceptible to easy misinterpretation. Many Bible prophecies are specific in their details, and the authentication and veracity of the prophet rests on them. The Scripture itself makes it clear that fulfilled prophecy is one of the evidences of the supernatural origin of the word of its prophets (Jer 28:9). Failure of fulfillment would unmask a false prophet: "You may say to yourselves, 'How can we know when a message has not been spoken by the LORD?' If what a prophet proclaims in the name of the LORD does not take place or come true, that is a message the LORD has not spoken. That prophet has spoken presumptuously. Do not be afraid of him" (Deut 18:21-22).

Isaiah ties the unmasking of false prophets to the failure of their predictive prophecy. "Bring in your idols to tell us what is going to happen. Tell us what the former things were, so that we may consider them and know their final outcome. Or declare to us the things to come, tell us what the future holds, so we may know that you are gods. Do something, whether good or bad, so that we will be dismayed and filled with fear" (Is 41:22-23).

There are various kinds of prophecies. One group has to do with predictions of a coming Messiah, the Lord Jesus Christ. Others have to do with specific historical events, and still others with the Jews. It is very significant that the early disciples quoted the Old Testament prophecies to show that Jesus fulfilled in detail the prophecies made many years earlier.

We can mention only a small but representative number of these prophecies. Our Lord refers to the predictive prophecies about himself in what must have been one of the most exciting Bible studies in history. After conversation with two disciples on the road to Emmaus, he said, " 'How foolish you are, and how slow of heart to believe all that the prophets have spoken! Did not the Christ have to suffer these things and then enter his glory?' And beginning with Moses and all the Prophets, he explained to them what was said in all the Scriptures concerning himself" (Lk 24:25-27).

Isaiah 52:13—53:12 is the most outstanding example of predictive prophecy about Christ. It's contingencies could not have been rigged in advance in an attempt to produce fulfillment. They involve his life, his rejection in ministry, his death, his burial and his reactions to the unjust judicial proceedings.

Micah 5:2 is a striking illustration of both a prediction about Christ and historic detail: "But you, Bethlehem Ephrathah, though you are small among the clans of Judah, out of you will come for me one who will be ruler over Israel, whose origins are from of old, from ancient times." It took a decree from the mighty Caesar Augustus himself to bring this historic event to pass.

Predictions dealt not only with the coming Messiah but with kings, nations and cities. Perhaps the most remarkable (Ezek 26) has to do with the city of Tyre. Here a whole series of little details are given as to how Tyre would be destroyed, the utter completeness of its destruction, and the fact that it would never be reconstructed (v. 4). How this prophecy was fulfilled by degrees in Nebuchadnezzar's attack and through the savage onslaught of Alex-

ander the Great, is a phenomenal illustration of the accurateness
and reality of predictive prophecy in the Bible.

Finally, there are the remarkable prophecies about the Jewish
people, the Israelites. Again, only a few of these startling prophecies may be cited.

Their dispersion was predicted by Moses and Hosea: "The LORD
will cause you to be defeated before your enemies. You will come
at them from one direction but flee from them in seven, and you
will become a thing of horror to all the kingdoms on earth" (Deut
28:25). "My God will reject them because they have not obeyed
him; they will be wanderers among the nations" (Hos 9:17). Persecution and contempt were predicted: "I will make them abhor-
rent and an offense to all the kingdoms of the earth, a reproach
and a byword, an object of ridicule and cursing, wherever I banish
them" (Jer 24:9). Jeremiah 31 makes the astonishing prediction of
the restoration of Israel as a nation. For centuries, this was considered to be unthinkable. Some events in our own time, however,
may well be at least partial fulfillment of these prophecies. All
observers agree that the reestablishment of Israel as a nation, in
1948, is one of the amazing political phenomena of our day.

One cannot deny the force of fulfilled prophecy. Especially since
many prophecies could not possibly have been written after the
events predicted.

The Holy Spirit's Role

There are, then, a number of pieces of evidence on which one can
reasonably base his or her belief that the Bible is the Word of God.
As helpful as these evidences are, the testimony of the Holy Spirit
is what finally makes one believe that the Bible is the Word of God.
As a person surveys the evidence and reads the Bible, "it dawns on
him," to use Gordon Clark's phrase, that the Bible is the Word of
God.[4] This realization is the work of the Holy Spirit. But the work
of the Spirit is always toward some purpose. This involves the

giving of *reasons* for belief, and the explanation of the Scripture message itself.

The two disciples on the road to Emmaus asked, "Were not our hearts burning within us?" (Lk 24:32). This same experience becomes ours as, with the Holy Spirit's help, we come to the conviction that the Bible is the Word of God, we feed on it and we share it with others.

For Individual and Group Study

1. Paul Little maintains that for the purpose of introducing a non-Christian to Jesus Christ and his claims, it is necessary only to prove that the Bible is made up of reliable historical documents (p. 62). Did you believe the Bible was *inspired* before you became a Christian or did you just think it was *reliable?* Explain.

How could you focus conversation with non-Christians on Christ's claims instead of their view of the Bible?

2. According to the scriptural use of the word *inspired,* how is the Bible's inspiration different from the inspiration of Shakespeare's plays?

3. How does Jesus' own view of the Old Testament Scriptures and of the prophetic powers of John the Baptist support the inspiration of the Bible?

4. Jesus demonstrated that he believed the Old Testament was God's Word. In what ways do you act on your belief that the Bible is God's Word?

5. Often when nonbelievers claim that Christians take the Bible too literally, what do they mean (pp. 65-66)?

Is this ever really a stumbling block for you? Why or why not?

6. The author suggests that a clear definition of *inerrancy* is needed (pp. 66-68). How would you define the term?

7. Fulfilled prophecy both validates the authenticity of the Old Testament documents and helps to prove Christ's claims (pp. 68-70). Would you use such an argument with one type of person more than another? Explain.

8. Consider the author's statement, "The testimony of the Holy Spirit is what finally makes one believe that the Bible is the Word of God" (p. 70). If you have experienced this (or have not), what was this experience like for you?

How does this affect your Christian life?

9. Practically speaking, why is it important to determine if the Bible is God's Word, his letter to the world?

10. What can we expect from a letter from God that we could not expect from any other manuscript?

11. Are there any ways you need to redirect your thinking in order to take the

Bible the way God intends it?

12. Take time now to add any new insights to your list of reasons for putting your hope in God through Christ Jesus. Space is provided after page 173.

For Further Reading

Carnell, Edward John. Chapters one through three and seven in *The Case for Orthodox Theology*. Philadelphia, Pa.: Westminster, 1959.

Lewis, C. S. "Modern Theology and Biblical Criticism" in *Christian Reflections*. Grand Rapids, Mich.: Eerdmans; London: Geoffrey Bles, 1967.

Stott, John R. W. *God's Book for God's People*. Downers Grove, Ill.: InterVarsity Press, 1982.

6
Are the Bible Documents Reliable?

● ● ● ● ● ● ● ● ● ● ●

SEVERAL YEARS AGO A LEADING MAGAZINE CARRIED AN ARTICLE purporting to show there are thousands of errors in the Bible.

How do we know that the text of the Bible as we have it today, having come to us through many translations and versions over the centuries, is not just a pale reflection of the original? What guarantee do we have that deletions and embellishments have not totally obscured the original message of the Bible? What difference does the historical accuracy of the Bible make? Surely the only thing that counts is the message!

But Christianity is rooted in history. Jesus Christ was counted in a Roman census. If the Bible's historical references are not true, grave questions may be raised about the reliability of other parts of the message based on historical events. Likewise, it is crucial for us to know that we have substantially the same documents in our time as people had almost 2,000 years ago. And how do we know the books we now have are the ones that should be in the Bible? or that others should not be included? These questions are worthy of answers.

If we believe the Bible to be the Word of God verbally inspired, the job of establishing the text accurately is an extremely important one. This task is called textual criticism. It has to do with the reliability of the text, i.e., how our current text compares with the originals and how accurately the ancient manuscripts were copied.

Who Wrote the Words?

Let us briefly examine the data for the Old and New Testaments.

It is evident that the work of a scribe was a highly professional and carefully executed task. It was also a task undertaken by a devout Jew with the highest devotion. Since he believed he was dealing with the Word of God, he was acutely aware of the need for extreme care and accuracy. There are no complete copies of the Hebrew Old Testament earlier than around A.D. 900, but it seems evident that the text was preserved very carefully and faithfully since at least A.D. 100 or 200.

A check is provided by comparing some translations from the Hebrew into Latin and Greek at about this time. This comparison reveals the careful copying of the Hebrew text during this period. The text dating from around A.D. 900 is called the "Masoretic Text" because it was the product of Jewish scribes known as the "Masoretes." All of the present copies of the Hebrew text which come from this period are in remarkable agreement, attesting to the skill of the scribes in proofreading.

But how could we know about the accuracy and authenticity of the text in pre-Masoretic times? The history of the Jews was very turbulent, raising questions as to the carefulness of the scribes during this hectic period.

The Dead Sea Scrolls

In 1947 the world learned about what has been called the greatest archeologic discovery of the century. In caves in the valley of the Dead Sea, ancient jars were discovered containing the now-famous Dead Sea Scrolls. From these scrolls, it is evident that a group of Jews lived at a place called Qumran from about 150 B.C. to A.D. 70.

Theirs was a communal society, operated very much like a monastery. In addition to tilling the fields, they spent their time studying and copying the Scriptures. It became apparent to them that the Romans were going to invade the land. They put their leather scrolls in jars and hid them in caves in the side of the cliffs west of the Dead Sea.

In the providence of God the scrolls survived undisturbed until discovered accidentally by a wandering Bedouin goat herdsman in February or March of 1947. The accidental discovery was followed by careful exploration, and then several other caves containing scrolls were found. The find included the earliest manuscript copy yet known of the complete Book of Isaiah, and fragments of almost every book in the Old Testament. In addition, there is a fragmented copy containing much of Isaiah 38—66. The Books of Samuel, in a tattered copy, were also found at that time, along with two complete chapters of Habakkuk. A number of nonbiblical items, including the rules of the ancient community, were also discovered.

The significance of this find, for those who wonder about the accuracy of the Old Testament text, can easily be seen. In one dramatic stroke, almost 1,000 years were hurdled in terms of the age of the manuscripts we now possess. By comparing the Dead Sea Scrolls with the Masoretic text, we would get a clear indication of the accuracy, or lack of it, of transmission over the period of nearly a millennium.

What was actually learned? In comparing the Qumran manuscript of Isaiah 38—66 with the one we had, scholars found that:

The text is extremely close to our Masoretic text. A comparison of Isaiah 53 shows that only seventeen letters differ from the Masoretic text. Ten of these are mere differences of spelling, like our "honor" or "honour" and produce no change in the meaning at all. Four more are very minor differences, such as the presence of the conjunction, which is often a matter of style. The other three letters are the Hebrew word for "light" which is added after "they shall see" in verse 11. Out of 166 words in this chapter, only this one word is really in question, and it does not at all change the sense of the passage. *This is typical of the whole manuscript.*[1]

The Septuagint

Other ancient witnesses attest the accuracy of the copyists who ultimately gave us the Masoretic text. One of these is the Greek translation of the Old Testament, called the Septuagint. It is often referred to as the LXX because it was reputedly done by seventy Jewish scholars in Alexandria. The best estimate of its date seems to be about the third century B.C.

Until the discovery of the Dead Sea Scrolls there was a question, when the LXX was different from the Masoretic text, why the variations existed. It is now apparent that the Masoretic text has not changed significantly since around 200 B.C. Other scrolls among those discovered show a type of Hebrew that is very similar to that from which the LXX was translated. The Samuel scroll especially resembles the reading of the LXX. The LXX appears to be a rather literal translation, and our manuscripts are pretty good copies of the original translation.

Another ancient witness is the evidence for a third type of text similar to that which was preserved by the Samaritans. Copies of the old scrolls of the Pentateuch are extant today in Nablus (Shechem), Palestine.

Three Families of Texts

Three main types of text existed in 200 B.C. The question for us is, What is the *original* version of the Old Testament, in the light of these three "families" of texts to choose from?

We can conclude with R. Laird Harris:

We can now be sure that copyists worked with great care and accuracy on the Old Testament, even back to 225 B.C. At that time there were two or three types of text available for copying. These types differed among themselves so little, however, that we can infer that still earlier copyists had also faithfully and carefully transmitted the Old Testament text. Indeed, it would be rash skepticism that would now deny that we have our Old Testament in a form very close to that used by Ezra when he taught the Law to those who had returned from the Babylonian captivity.[2]

New Testament Documents

Again, based on the evidence, the conviction comes that we have in our hands a text which does not differ in any substantial particular from the originals of the various books as they came from the hands of the human writer. The great scholar F. J. A. Hort said that apart from insignificant variations of grammar or spelling, not more than one-thousandth part of the whole New Testament is affected by differences of reading.[3]

The New Testament was written in Greek. More than 6,000 manuscripts of the New Testament, or parts of it, have survived to our time. These are on different materials. Papyrus was the common material used for writing purposes at the beginning of the Christian era. It was made from reeds and was highly durable. In the last 500 years many remains of documents written on papyrus have been discovered, including fragments of manuscripts of the New Testament.

The second material of which Greek manuscripts were made is

parchment. This was the skin of sheep or goats, polished with pumice. It was used until the late Middle Ages, when paper began to replace it.

The dates of the New Testament documents indicate that they were written within the lifetime of contemporaries of Christ. People were still alive who could remember the things he said and did. Many of the Pauline letters are even earlier than some of the Gospels.[4]

The evidence for the early existence of the New Testament writings is clear. The wealth of materials for the New Testament becomes even more evident when we compare it with other ancient documents which have been accepted without question. Bruce observes that only nine or ten good manuscripts of Caesar's *Gallic War* exist. The oldest of these manuscripts was written some 900 years after Caesar's time. The *History of Thucydides* (ca. 460-400 B.C.) is known to us from eight manuscripts, the earliest belonging to around A.D. 900, and a few papyrus scraps that belong to about the beginning of the Christian era. The same is true of the *History of Herodotus* (ca. 480-425 B.C.). However, no classical scholar would listen to an argument that the authenticity of Herodotus or Thucydides is in doubt because of the earliest manuscripts of their work which are of any use to us are more than 1,300 years later than the originals.[5]

By contrast there are two excellent manuscripts of the New Testament from the fourth century. Fragments of papyrus copies of books of the New Testament date from 100 to 200 years earlier still. Perhaps the earliest piece of data we have is a fragment of a papyrus codex containing John 18:31-33, 37. It is dated around A.D. 130.

More Evidence

The authenticity of the New Testament comes from other sources. These are the references and quotations of the New Testament books by both friends and enemies of Christianity. The Apostolic Fathers, writing mostly between A.D. 90 and 160, give indication of familiarity with most of the books of the New Testament.

It seems apparent, from recent discoveries, that the Gnostic school of Valentinus was also familiar with most of the New Testament.[6]

There are two other sources of data for establishing the authenticity of the New Testament books. The first source is the versions. Versions are those manuscripts which were translated from the Greek into other languages. Three groups of these are of the most significance: the Syriac versions, the Egyptian or Coptic versions and the Latin versions. By careful study of the versions, important clues have been uncovered as to the original Greek manuscripts from which they were translated.

Finally, there is the evidence of the lectionaries, the reading lessons used in public church services. By the middle of the twentieth century more than 1,800 of these reading lessons had been classified. There are lectionaries of the Gospels, the Acts and the Epistles. Though they did not appear before the sixth century, the text from which they quote may itself be early and of high quality.[7]

Though there have been many changes in the many copyings of the New Testament writings, most of them are minor. The science of textual criticism, which is very exacting, has enabled us to be sure of the true text of the New Testament.

Rather than share the alarm and skepticism of published accounts of biblical "errors," we can rest with the conclusion of the late Sir Frederic Kenyon, a world-renowned scholar of the ancient manuscripts. He said: "The interval, then, between the dates of original composition and the earliest extant evidence becomes so small as to be in fact negligible, and the last foundation for any doubt that the Scriptures have come down to us substantially as they were written has now been removed. Both the authenticity and the general integrity of the books of the New Testament may be regarded as finally established."[8]

The Question of the Canon

A question closely allied to that of the reliability of the texts we have is, How do we know the books in our Bible, and no others, are the ones that should be there? This is called the question of the canon. There are distinct questions involved for Old and New Testaments.

The Protestant church accepts identically the same Old Testament books as the Jews had, and as Jesus and the apostles accepted. The Roman Catholic church, since the Council of Trent in 1546, includes the books of the Apocrypha. The order in the English Bible follows that of the Septuagint. This is different from the Hebrew Bible, in which the books are divided into three groups: the Law (Genesis to Deuteronomy), known also as the Torah or the Pentateuch; the Prophets, including the Former Prophets (Joshua, Judges, Samuel, Kings) and the Latter Prophets (Isaiah, Jeremiah, Ezekiel and the Book of the Twelve—Hosea to Malachi); and the Writings, the remaining books of our Old Testament canon.

The books were received as authoritative because they were recognized as utterances of people inspired by God to reveal his Word. As E. J. Young says:

When the Word of God was written, it became Scripture, and inasmuch as it had been spoken by God, it possessed absolute authority. Since it was the Word of God, it was canonical. That which determines the canonicity of a book, therefore, is the fact that the book is inspired of God. Hence, a distinction is properly made between the authority which the Old Testament books possess as divinely inspired and the recognition of that authority on the part of Israel.[9]

We can see this development in the work of Moses. The laws issued by him and by the later prophets were intended to be respected as the decrees of God himself. They were so regarded then and also by later generations. The Law was neglected, to be sure, but its authority was recognized by Israel's spiritual leaders. It was the recognition of this authority that shook Josiah when he realized how long the Law had been neglected (2 Kings 22:11).

When we examine the writings of the prophets, it is obvious that they believed they spoke with authority. "This is what the Lord says" and "the word of the Lord came to me" are common preambles to their messages.

It is not clear on what grounds the authority of the writings was accepted. That it *was* accepted, however, *is* clear. In New Testament times it was customary to describe at least some of these writings as the utterances of the Holy Spirit.

By the beginning of the Christian era the term *Scripture* had come to mean a fixed body of divinely inspired writings that were fully recognized as authoritative. Our Lord used the term in this sense and was fully understood by his hearers when he said, "The Scripture cannot be broken" (Jn 10:35). It is interesting that there was no controversy between our Lord and the Pharisees on the authority of the Old Testament. Contention arose because they gave *tradition* the same authority as Scripture.

At the Council of Jamnia, in A.D. 90, informal discussions were held about the canon. Whether any formal or binding decisions were made is problematic. The discussion seemed to center not on whether certain books should be included in the canon, but whether certain ones should be excluded. In any case, those present recognized what already was accepted. They did not bring into being what had not previously existed. In other words, they recognized but did not *establish* the canonicity of the Old Testament books as we have them.

The Apocryphal Books

The apocryphal books, it is important to note, were never received into the Jewish canon and were not considered as part of the inspired Scriptures by Jews or Christians in the early centuries of the Christian era. This is evident from a study of the writings of Josephus, the Jewish historian, and of Augustine, the great North African Bishop of Hippo.

It is interesting that the New Testament writers do not once quote the Apocrypha.

The apocryphal books do not claim to be the Word of God or the work of prophets. They vary greatly in content and value. Some, like 1 Maccabees, were probably written around 100 B.C. and are valuable as historical background. Others are more characterized by legend and are of little value. Though not included at first, these books were later added to the LXX. In this way they came to be included by Jerome in the Latin Vulgate. Even Jerome, however, accepted only the books in the Hebrew Canon. He viewed the others as having ecclesiastical value only. He was in conflict with the later action of the Council of Trent, in Reformation times, which elevated the Apocrypha to canonical status.

For the Old Testament we have, ultimately, the witness of our Lord to the canonicity of the thirty-nine books we now have.

What about the New Testament?

Here, as for the Old Testament, the books possessed canonicity by virtue of their inspiration, not by virtue of their being voted into canonicity by any group. The history of the recognition of the New Testament's canonicity, however, is interesting. Much of the material of the New Testament claimed apostolic authority. Paul and Peter clearly wrote with this authority in mind. Peter specifically refers to Paul's letters as Scripture (2 Pet 3:15-16).

Jude (v. 18) says that 2 Peter 3:3 is a word from the apostles. Such early church fathers as Polycarp, Ignatius and Clement mention a number of the New Testament books as authoritative.

The onslaught of heresy in the middle of the second century caused the concept of a canon to be revived in the thinking of

Christians. What was authoritative and what was not came to be clearly delineated. Irenaeus and later Eusebius, in the third century, give us more light in their writings. The final fixation of the canon as we know it came in the fourth century. In the East, a letter of Athanasius in A.D. 367 clearly distinguishes between works in the canon which are described as the sole sources of religious instruction and others which believers were permitted to read. In the West, the canon was fixed by decision of a church council held at Carthage in A.D. 397.

Three criteria were generally used throughout this period of time to establish that particular written documents were the true record of the voice and message of apostolic witness. First, could authorship be attributed to an apostle? The Gospels of Mark and Luke do not meet this criterion specifically, but were accepted as the works of close associates of the apostles. Second, there was the matter of ecclesiastical usage—that is, recognition of a book by a leading church or majority of churches. Third, there was conformity to standards of sound doctrine.

These data are helpful and interesting, but in the final analysis, as with the question of the inspiration of the Scripture, canonicity is a question of the witness of the Spirit in the hearts of God's people.

In days of uncertainty, what a rock the Scripture is on which to stand! "Heaven and earth will pass away," says our Lord, "but my words will never pass away" (Lk 21:33).

For Individual and Group Study

1. The earliest existing manuscript of Caesar's *Gallic War* was copied nine hundred years after Caesar's time—five hundred years more than the gap between the earliest complete New Testament and its original texts. Why do historians accept the reliability of Caesar's *Gallic War* while the average person questions the reliability of the Bible?

2. How do the Dead Sea Scrolls and multiple versions of Scripture (pp. 75-77) help historians say, with R. Laird Harris: "Indeed, it would be rash skepticism that

would now deny that we have our Old Testament in a form very close to that used by Ezra when he taught the law to those who had returned from the Babylonian captivity" (p. 77)?

3. A second problem in determining the Old Testament's reliability is determining which books rightly belong in the canon (pp. 80-82). What light does Christ's use of Old Testament Scripture shed on the Old Testament's authenticity?

4. Problems in New Testament reliability do not rest on lack of early manuscripts. However, we do not have Christ's "stamp of acceptance" on the books we include in the canon because they were written after his ascension (pp. 82-83). What is the evidence in favor of the reliability of New Testament books?

5. Which questions concerning the reliability of the Bible seem most troublesome to you or people you know? Why?

6. Which answers offered in this chapter help resolve questions for you? What questions still remain unanswered in your mind?

7. If you have unanswered questions that seem important enough to pursue further, where could you go for help resolving them?

8. Take time now to add any new insights to your list of reasons for putting your hope in God through Christ Jesus. Space is provided following page 173.

For Further Reading

Bruce, F. F. *The New Testament Documents: Are They Reliable?* Downers Grove, Ill.: InterVarsity Press, 1981.

Carnell, Edward John. Chapters one through three and seven in *The Case for Orthodox Theology*. Philadelphia, Pa.: Westminster, 1959.

Lewis, C. S. "Modern Theology and Biblical Criticism" in *Christian Reflections*. Grand Rapids, Mich.: Eerdmans; London: Geoffrey Bles, 1967.

Stott, John R. W. *God's Book for God's People*. Downers Grove, Ill.: InterVarsity Press, 1982.

7
Does Archaeology Verify Scripture?

● ● ● ● ● ● ● ● ● ●

I N THE EARLY YEARS OF THE NINETEENTH CENTURY, A NEW DOOR of information opened to the earliest roots of the human race in the Near East. Increased travel and exploration provided the hinges to the door, and modern archaeologists walked through in a spurt of enthusiasm. They began to dig below the earth's surface for the material remains of humankind's past found in ancient palaces, buried temples and animal stables. Civilizations came alive that existed long before the known world of Greece. Babylon (called "great") where Daniel lived revealed double walls with nine ornamented gates. Egypt showed marvels of painted tombs, bandaged mummies, mirrors, perfume jars and mascara pots.

At first the buried cultures themselves were the objects of study. Then there appeared places and names from the Old Testament on palace walls. Names of Assyrian tyrants that warred with Israel, along with their armies and hapless captives, were found. Persian governors spoke through their letters. The Pharaohs of Egypt, some lying in solid gold coffins, could now be identified.

In the wake of these discoveries, biblical scholars found rich background for the biblical history of Israel and her neighbors. The historical and geographic reliability of the Bible was affirmed in a number of important areas. This was in marked contrast to the centuries before when there was little evidence to corroborate the Bible's historical statements. Critics would dismiss the narratives by casting them as implausible stories set in fictional backgrounds rather than genuine historical events. But by the middle of this century it began to be recognized that archaeological discoveries were substantiating the biblical record. The statements of well-known authorities who were not evangelicals are indicative of this. Dr. W. F. Albright, late professor emeritus of Johns Hopkins University, could declare, "There can be no doubt that archeology has confirmed the substantial historicity of Old Testament tradition."[1]

Millar Burrows of Yale stated:

On the whole, however, archaeological work has unquestionably strengthened confidence in the reliability of the scriptural record. More than one archaeologist has found his respect for the Bible increased by the experience of excavation in Palestine.[2] Archaeology has in many cases refuted the views of modern critics. It has shown, in a number of instances, that these views rest on false assumptions and unreal, artificial schemes of historical development. This is a real contribution and not to be minimized.[3]

The help from archaeology falls roughly into two categories. First, it has verified some specific biblical events that were doubted and even ridiculed. (One scholar observed that it is a rare passage that has not been questioned by someone.) The second category of help is more general in nature in filling in overall background to the culture and practices of the biblical times. Such things as economic problems and literary development describe the world to which the Old Testament prophets spoke. Note examples later in this chapter.

It is evident that certain points of apparent conflict between the biblical record and the information previously available have been cleared up as more information has been obtained. It would seem, then, that when apparent conflicts still exist, rather than conclude that the Bible must be wrong, it would seem much more reasonable to admit the problem exists and to hold it open pending further discoveries.

Having said all this, however, it is important to point out that we cannot prove the Bible by archaeology, nor do we believe the Bible on the basis of archaeological proof. H. Darrell Lance writes to this: "Although archaeology can sometimes provide independent evidence for the existence of certain places, persons or events mentioned in the Bible, it can say nothing at all about whether God had anything to do with any of it. That, for the modern believer as well as for the ancient Israelite, is a matter of faith."[4]

Added to faith, it is the Holy Spirit who ultimately confirms the truth of the Scripture to us. Spiritual truth can never be confirmed by archaeology. But we can be thankful for the historical details which have been confirmed by archaeology even though we recognize the apparent conflicts that still exist.

Sources of the Archaeologist

More than 25,000 sites showing some connection with the Old Testament period have been located in Bible lands. Yet there is still a wealth of material that awaits discovery. Throughout the Near East mounds of earth and debris (called "tells") mark the places where towns or cities once flourished. Most of the major cities of the Bible can be identified, A. R. Millard states, either by "general geographical considerations or by tradition (though that may not be very reliable) or by current use of the ancient name."[5] A major example of this latter situation is the city of Damascus. It has existed under that name 3,500 years or more.

The largest body of evidence for comparison with Scriptures is found in the ancient Eastern inscriptions. Few contemporary documents from Old Testament times have been found in Palestine. Illustrations must be drawn from the writings of neighboring countries.

Another major source of information for comparison with biblical narratives has been the archaeological excavation of biblical sites.

The field of information and correlation with biblical data is so vast that we can spotlight only a few of the major contributions.

How Can These Finds Be Dated?

The ancient cities were built and rebuilt in the same place, so that a whole succession of levels is usually found, the lowest of course, being the oldest. The question arises, how can these finds be dated? Fashions in pottery changed, and if at one excavated site a particular fashion can be dated, the similar pottery found elsewhere will obviously be of the same period. Kings often inscribed their names on the hinge-sockets of temple doors, and the name of their god would be given. Inscribed stones were often laid under palace or temple walls in memory of the founder. Royal sepulchers can usually be identified in the same way.

Archaeologists have uncovered copies of lists dating back almost 2000 B.C. They were drawn up by Sumerian scribes cataloging the kings according to their successive dynasties with notes as to the lengths of their reigns. A few miles from Ur an inscribed foundation stone was found, laid by a king of unknown name, of the First Dynasty of Ur, which the scribes speak of as the third dynasty after the Flood. This king apparently reigned 3,100 years before Christ and more than a thousand years before Abraham.[6]

A. R. Millard observed:

Archaeologists usually concentrate on the more rewarding parts, where temples or palaces stood, or lay out their trenches to probe each period of existence in the life of the place. To do this a trench may slice right through the mound, producing a small amount of information at all levels. Any area of especial interest can be marked and explored with a larger trench. Each building or time of occupation will have left its mark on the mound in the form of floor surfaces, stumps of walls, and heaps of rubbish. These will be sandwiched between earlier remains below and later remains above.[7]

Abraham's Time

A good example of the help archaeology can be to us comes from the life and times of Abraham. The critics claimed the culture pictured in the Genesis story did not correlate with their knowledge of Near Eastern life up to that time. However, a change came when in 1933 a party of Arabs were digging a grave by the River Euphrates. They unearthed a stone statue and reported their find. Soon a team of archaeologists dug out other statues and eventually unearthed an elaborate palace bearing the name of the city of Mari. The royal palace covered more than six acres and had over 260 rooms, courtyards and passages.

Millard describes the palace as containing rooms with walls fifteen feet high, some empty and some filled with jars that stood ready for oil, wine or grain. There were spacious living quarters for the king, his wives and his family; and more cramped ones for officials and servants. One can imagine craftsmen in workshops, cooks in the kitchens, secretaries, servants and singing troupes for the king's entertainment. One of the many statues found was of a bearded man dating from the eighteenth century B.C. and inscribed with the name Ishtupilum, King of Mari.

Some 20,000 cuneiform (wedge-shaped writing) tablets from royal archives were found. Accountants had used some of the tablets to record grain, vegetables and other provisions brought into the palace. Letters to the king, musical instruments and gold for decorations are all mentioned. There are even letters with messages from prophets to gods. A jar of buried treasure and inscriptions date the city around 2500 B.C., and since Abraham is variously thought to be in the same general era between the nineteenth and twentieth centuries B.C., this is certainly the kind of culture in which he lived.

The tablets of another city, Nuzi, situated east of the city of Mari near the Tigris River, details some of the social customs of the city in the fourteenth and fifteenth centuries B.C. Families are described in situations similar to the dilemma Abraham faced in Genesis 15:4 when he took Ishmael as his own son. If later the couple had a natural child, the adopted son would have to yield some of his rights to the second son.[8]

The Nuzi tablets recall another similar incident to Genesis 16:1-2 where Sarah presents her handmaid Hagar to Abraham to bear a child. Yamauchi tells us of a "tablet of adoption which stipulates that a barren wife must provide a slave girl to her husband to beget a son. This particular tablet and the Hammurabi Law Code require that the slave's child be kept—a rule which was preempted by the divine command to send Hagar and Ishmael away."[9]

One other Syrian site, Alalakh on the Orontes River, describes a husband who mistreated a wife (literally "drags her by the nose") and so had to give up his wife, her dowry and the bridal gift which he had presented to her family.[10]

The impact of the cities of Mari, Nuzi and Alalakh lies in the information they provide of ancient civilizations, giving clues of what went on in Syria and Mesopotamia historically and politically. In addition we get a new view into the urban lifestyles and its sharp contrast with the pastoral life known from the Patriarchal narratives.

These records cover a broad spectrum from business, politics, government and the arts. They reflect customs and social relationships that parallel the situations that the biblical patriarchs faced. When we see Abraham in the settings similar to those known from the cities of Mari and Nuzi, the biblical accounts become highly credible and believable. The life and history, the political movements, the cultural and business activities of these two cities all paint a wonderfully illuminated background of the world of the father of the Hebrew nation.

Writing in the Patriarchal Times

Did you ever wonder about the literary abilities of the Patriarchs? The bustling city of Ebla provides the largest early archive thus far unearthed from the New East. It dated back to the third millennium B.C. Although its existence had been known, its location and highly developed culture was unsuspected. The city was divided into two sectors, an acropolis and a lower city. The upper division contained four building complexes, including the palace of the king, temple to the goddess Ishtar and numerous stables. The lower section was divided into four quarters boasting four gates.

In a room adjacent to the temple, archaeologists found an astonishing collection of more than 20,000 tablets on the floor. The small room had been burned. In the heat of the flames the brickwork was baked, and the tablets as well. As a result both room and tablets withstood the ravages of the centuries until they were uncovered in 1975. History has been preserved for 5,000 years![11]

Years of research will yet be required to interpret these vast records. But one of the valuable contributions of these tablets lies in the evidence they provide that cuneiform writing had spread to north Syria before 2300 B.C. It also shows the habit of recording every sort of activity, business and cultural. Dictionaries confirm the presence of west Semitic people of other languages in that era. Biblical history, we now know, took place in a world where writing was well established.

The Biblical Kings

Archaeology has given us colorful background information for the study of the biblical kings. Solomon's grandeur has been the target of special skepticism. His lavish wealth is described in 1 Kings 9—10 as consisting of a royal navy built on the shore of the Red Sea even though there is no suitable harbor on the coastline of Palestine. His army had use of 1,400 chariots and 1,200 horses. His building projects were extensive, including fortification of the cities of Jerusalem, Hazor, Megiddo and Gezer (9:15). Recent excavation at these last three cities have at least documented Solomon's building skills.

In 1960 the famed Israeli scholar Yigael Yadin, while excavating the city of Megiddo, had identified the layer of Solomon's time by comparing pottery types. Knowing that 1 Kings 9:15 grouped together the three cities of Megiddo, Hazor and Gezer as being built by Solomon, he had a sudden inspiration. He recalled the Megiddo Gate from Solomon's time had three chambers on each side. Could the other two cities be the same? He tells this exciting story of the dig at Hazor:

> Before proceeding further with the excavation of Hazor, we made tentative markings on the ground following our estimate of the plan of the gate on the basis of the Megiddo Gate. And then we told the laborers to go ahead and continue removing the debris. When they had finished, they looked at us with astonishment, as if we were magicians or fortunetellers. For there, before us, was the gate whose outline we had marked a replica of the Megiddo Gate. This proved not only that both gates had been built by Solomon but that both had followed a single master plan.[12]

Solomon's Gold

First Kings 10:21 adds the information that Solomon possessed large stores of precious metals. The temple he built for the Lord, like the golden shrine of King Tutankhaman of Egypt, was a glory of gold as described in the latter half of 1 Kings 6. "Solomon covered the inside of the temple with pure gold, and he extended gold chains across the front of the inner sanctuary, which was overlaid with gold. So he overlaid the whole interior with gold" (6:21-22). The whole concept is breathtaking.

Although the exact site of Solomon's Temple has not been found, other discoveries showed that kings of surrounding nations of his time possessed technology and workmanship similar to the biblical account. Millard elaborates:

> Extravagant as this may seem, a display of gold was a matter of pride for any powerful ruler (i.e., valuable plates are displayed at royal banquets today). National currency reserves were held in gold, not stored idly in bank vaults to be publicized merely as figures, but shown to the populace. When a stronger army attacked, the gold was stripped and handed over (cf. 2 Kings 18:16). Assyrian, Babylonian, and Egyptian monarchs boast of the gold they donated to beautify temples in their own cities. Their inscriptions speak of walls "covered with gold like plaster," of doors and doorways carved in relief and plated with gold, of furniture and decorations sheathed in precious metal. One Assyrian king seized six decorative golden shields from a temple in Armenia, each weighing twelve times as much as each of the shields Solomon hung in his palace (1 Kings 10:16-17; cf. 14:26-27). Claims of pompous emperors may be treated as grossly inflated, but with these uses of gold that is not so. Small fragments of thin gold sheets have been found in Assyria and Babylonia, and in Egypt nail holes . . . for attaching the metal are visible in . . . stonework.[13]

At least one of the sources of Solomon's gold came from Ophir. First Kings 9:11, as well as other passages, describes Hiram, king of Tyre, as supplying Solomon "with all the cedar and pine and gold he wanted." And verse 28 tells of Hiram's men who "sailed to Ophir and brought back 420 talents of gold, which they delivered to King Solomon." Although this city's exact location still remains a mystery (with conjectures ranging from the Samali coast of Africa to India), its existence and assets have been independently attested. A potsherd from the mid-eighth century B.C. has been unearthed at a port north of Tel Aviv. It carried the clear notation of the contents marked by a local clerk saying, "Ophir gold for Beth-Horon: 30 shekels" (about 340 g., 12 oz.).[14]

One conclusion can be safely made: Solomon's golden temple was no mere invention of exaggerating scribes. It falls into the known patterns of ancient practices of his times.

A Conflict Described

Some of the objects unearthed by archaeologists give very specific details of biblical events. One example of this is a stone memorial telling of a conflict between Moab and Israel. The Bible notes that after Ahab died, Mesha, the king of Moab, and his people rebelled against Israel's rule over them and refused to pay tribute. A battle raged between Moab and the kings of Israel, Judah and Edom. The pressure of battle was so great that in desperation Mesha offered his eldest son on the wall as a burnt offering to the god of the Moabites, Chemosh. What happened then is not clear, but the implication is that the three kings had to abandon their siege against Moab.

In an 1868 excavation a German named Klein found an inscribed stone at Dibon, the land of Moab. Since the stone was owned by Arabs living at Dibon, he returned home to raise money for its purchase. The Arabs, thinking they could get a higher price for it, roasted the stone and then threw cold water over it to break it in pieces. Fortunately, Klein had taken an impression of the intact stone, so it was possible to restore the fragments and translate them after its purchase. It is now at the Louvre in Paris. In an early form of the Phoenician alphabet, the inscription describes how

Mesha, king of Moab, with the help of his god Chemosh, had thrown off the rule of Israel. King Omri of Israel, Ahab's father, is referred to by name in the inscription and a number of biblical place-names mentioned. Significantly, it mentions the God of Israel, called Yahweh.[15]

Daniel and Belshazzar

From a host of other discoveries, Daniel's account of the irreverent King Belshazzar stands out. Daniel names Belshazzar as the last king of Babylon. Yet all known Babylonian records listed Nabonidus as the last king. An obvious discrepancy, the critics cried! Then it was discovered in a Babylonian chronicle that Nabonidus inexplicably removed himself for a ten-year stint in Arabia, leaving the kingdom in the hands of his son Belshazzar. The confusion came because Nabonidus did not abdicate the kingship. He was still called king. Although Belshazzar was not the sole king, Daniel and the Hebrew young men with him considered him as the de facto king. Prior to the study of the Babylonian chronicles, Belshazzar was mentioned only in the biblical record. The archaeologist R. F. Dougherty concludes after his study of these findings: "Of all non-Babylonian records dealing with the situation at the close of the Neo-Babylonian Empire, [the description of events in] . . . Daniel [5] ranks next to cuneiform literature in accuracy."[16]

New Testament Research

Archaeological research and discovery for the New Testament has been of a different nature than for the Old. It is not so much a matter of digging for buried buildings or inscribed tablets; rather, New Testament archaeology is primarily a matter of written documents.

F. F. Bruce comments:

These documents may be public or private inscriptions on stone or some equally durable material: they may be papyri recovered from the sand of Egypt recording literary texts or housewives' shopping lists; they may be private notes scratched on fragments of unglazed pottery; they may be legends on coins preserving information about some otherwise forgotten ruler or getting some point of official propaganda across to the people who used them. They may represent a Christian church's collection of sacred Scriptures, like the Chester Beatty Biblical Papyri; they may be all that is left of the library of an ancient religious community, like the scrolls from Qumran or the Gnostic texts from Nag Hammadi. But whatever their character, they can be as important and relevant for the study of the New Testament as any cuneiform tablets are for the study of the Old.[17]

Papyrus documents have yielded a wealth of information. The common people wrote letters on papyrus and kept the ordinary commercial accounts of life on it. An even cheaper writing material was broken pieces of pottery, called *ostraca.* These were used for odd notes. One of the great significances of these materials, discovered in ancient rubbish heaps, has been to show the connection between the everyday language of the common people and the Greek in which most of the New Testament is written. It has long been recognized that there are great differences between the Greek of classic literature and that of the New Testament. Some scholars went so far as to suggest that New Testament Greek was a heavenly language which came into being for the purpose of recording Christian revelation. But through the discoveries of the papyri it became evident that the New Testament Greek was very similar to the language of the common people.

In 1931 the discovery of a collection of papyrus texts of the Greek Scriptures was made public. They have come to be known as the "Chester Beatty Biblical Papyri." F. F. Bruce says that this collection evidently formed the Bible of some outlying church in Egypt; it comprises eleven fragmentary codices. Three of these, in their complete state, contained most of the New Testament. One contained the Gospels and Acts, another Paul's nine letters to churches and the Epistle to the Hebrews, and a third the Revelation. All three were written in the third century. The Pauline codex, oldest of the three, was written at the beginning of that century. Even in their present mutilated state, these papyri bear most important testimony to the early textual history of the New Testament.[18] In addition, there is the oldest known fragment of any part of the New Testament from a codex of St. John's Gospel dated around A.D. 130.

Stone Inscriptions

Inscriptions on stone have been another source of valuable information. An example of this is an edict of Claudius inscribed on limestone at Delphi in central Greece. "This edict is to be dated [as originating] during the first seven months of A.D. 52, and mentions Gallio as being proconsul of Achaia. We know from other sources that Gallio's proconsulship lasted only for a year, and since proconsuls entered on their term of office on July 1, the inference is that Gallio entered on his proconsulship on that date in A.D. 51. But Gallio's proconsulship of Achaia overlapped Paul's year and a half of ministry in Corinth (Acts 18:11-12) so that Claudius' inscription provides us with a fixed point for reconstructing the chronology of Paul's career."[19]

Luke makes so many specific references to people and places that his writings are more easily illustrated by this kind of material than other parts of the New Testament. His accuracy of detail has been thoroughly established. Where he has been questioned, new evidence has vindicated him a number of times. Bruce points out:

> For example, his reference in Luke 3:1 to "Lysanias, the tetrarch of Abilene," at the time when John the Baptist began his ministry A.D. 27 has been regarded as a mistake because the only ruler of that name in those parts known from ancient historians was King Lysanias, whom Antony executed at Cleopatra's insti-

gation in 36 B.C. But a Greek inscription from Abila (eighteen miles west-northwest of Damascus), from which the territory of Abilene is named, records a dedication to one Nymphaeus "freeman of Lysanias, the tetrarch" between A.D. 14-29, around the very time indicated by Luke.[20]

No Pious Forgery

Coins have provided some background information for parts of New Testament history. One of the crucial questions in establishing the chronology of Paul's career is the date of Felix's replacement by Festus as procurator of Judea (Acts 24:27). A new Judean coinage began in Nero's fifth year, before October of A.D. 59. This may point to the beginning of the new procuratorship.

Some sacred sites have been definitely identified and general locations have also been uncovered. General locations have been more easily established than exact spots where some of the great New Testament events transpired.

Jerusalem was destroyed in A.D. 70 and a new pagan city was founded on the site in A.D. 135. This has complicated the identification of places in Jerusalem mentioned in the Gospels and Acts. Some, however, like the temple area and the Pool of Siloam, to which our Lord sent the blind man to wash (Jn 9:11), have been clearly identified.

Archeology is a real help in understanding the Bible. It yields fascinating information which illuminates what might otherwise be obscured and in some instances confirms what some might otherwise regard as doubtful.

We can agree with Keith N. Schoville who says: "It is important to realize that archaeological excavations have produced ample evidence to prove unequivocally that the Bible is not a pious forgery. Thus far, no historical statement in the Bible has been proven false on the basis of evidence retrieved through archaeologic research."[21]

For Individual or Group Study

1. Of the archaeological findings mentioned in this chapter, which did you find to be most interesting and impressive? Explain your answer.

2. It stands to reason that if the Bible is true, archaeology could only substantiate biblical claims. Why were Christians once fearful of the archaeologist's pick?

3. When do archaeologists find "errors" in the biblical accounts (pp. 86-87)?

4. As far as proving the Bible's accuracy, what are the limitations of archaeology (p. 87)?

5. What does it do to your faith to hear that archaeology substantiates Scripture?

6. When talking to a nonbeliever about the claims of Christ, would you mention archaeological findings that concern Scripture? Why or why not?

7. Some years ago, a rumor was widely published that scientists had proven that the earth had stopped its rotation for a day—the same amount of time that Joshua 10 tells us Joshua asked God to extend daylight so Israel could fight a key battle. The rumor turned out to be wishful thinking, but it showed people's desire to prove the *supernatural* aspects of Scripture. Do you ever have this desire? Why or why not?

8. Do you think such evidence would really make a difference to those who do not yet believe?

9. Take time now to add any new insights to your list of reasons for putting your hope in God through Christ Jesus. Space is provided following page 173.

For Further Reading

Bruce, F. F. "Archaeological Confirmation of the New Testament" in *Revelation and the Bible*. C. F. Henry, ed. Grand Rapids, Mich.: Baker Book House, 1958.

Schoville, Keith N. *Biblical Archaeology in Focus*. Grand Rapids, Mich.: Baker Book House, 1978.

Yamauchi, Edwin M. *The Stones and the Scripture*. Philadelphia, Pa.; New York: Lippencott, 1972.

8
Are Miracles Possible?

• • • • • • • • • •

DO YOU REALLY BELIEVE JONAH WAS SWALLOWED BY A WHALE? And do you seriously think that Christ *actually* fed 5,000 persons from five loaves of bread and two fish?" So goes the trend and tone of many modern questioners. Surely, they say, these "miracle" stories in the Bible must be quaint ways of conveying spiritual truth, and they are not meant to be taken literally.

With many questions, it is more important to discern the root problem than to become involved in discussing a twig on a branch. This is especially true of questions about miracles. The questioner's problem is generally not with a particular miracle, but with a whole principle. To establish the miracle in question would not answer his question. His controversy is with the whole principle of the possibility of miracles.

The Whole Concept of God

One who has problems with miracles often has difficulty with the validity of predictive prophecy. These questions stem from a weak view of God. The real problem is not with miracles or prophecy, but with the whole concept of God. Once we assume the existence of God, there is no problem with miracles, because God is by definition all-powerful. In the absence of such a God, however, the concept of miracles becomes difficult, if not impossible, to entertain.

This came to me very forcibly one day as I was talking about the deity of Christ with a Japanese professor friend. "I find it very difficult to believe," he said, "that a man could become God." Sensing his problem, I replied, "Yes, Kinichi, so do I, but I can believe that God became a man." He saw the difference in a flash, and not long afterward he became a Christian.

God Is Not Bound by Natural Law

The question, then, really is, "Does an all-powerful God, who created the universe, exist?" If so, we shall have little difficulty with miracles in which he transcends the natural law of which he is the author. It is important to keep this fundamental question in mind in discussing miracles. How we know God exists has already been discussed.

David Hume and others have defined a miracle as a violation of natural law. To take such a position, however, is practically to deify natural law, to capitalize it in such a way that whatever God there may be becomes the prisoner of natural law and, in effect, ceases to be God.

In this modern scientific age, people tend to personify science and natural law. They fail to realize that these are merely the impersonal results of observation. A Christian believes in natural law, which is to say that things behave in a certain cause-and-effect way almost all the time—year after year, century after century. But in maintaining this he does not restrict God's right and power to intervene when and how he chooses. God is over, above and outside natural law, and is not bound by it.

Laws do not *cause* anything in the sense that God causes things. They are merely descriptions of what happens.

What, in Fact, Is a Miracle?

We use the term rather loosely today. If a scared student passes an exam, he says, "It was a miracle!" Or if an old jalopy makes a successful trip from one city to another, we say, "It's a miracle the thing ran!" We use the term to mean anything that is unusual or unexpected. We do not necessarily mean that the hand of God has been at work.

In a consideration of miracles as they are thought of in the Bible, however, the word is used in an entirely different sense. Here we mean an act of God breaking into, changing, or interrupting the ordinary course of things.

To be sure, the Bible records various kinds of miracles, and some of them *could* have a *natural* explanation. For instance, the parting of the Red Sea was accomplished by the *natural* cause of the high winds which drove the waters back. Perhaps this *could* have happened apart from God's intervention. The miraculous part was the timing. That the waters should part just as the Israelites reached the shore, and should close on the Egyptians as they were in hot pursuit, and after every Israelite was safely on dry land, clearly proves the miraculous intervention of God.

On the other hand, there are many miracles for which there are no *natural* explanations. The resurrection of Lazarus from the dead and the resurrection of our Lord involved forces unknown to us and outside the realm of so-called natural law. The same is true with many of the miraculous healings. It has been fashionable to explain these in terms of psychosomatic response. We know today that many illnesses, rather than having an organic origin, originate in the mind. If the mental condition is corrected, the physical condition rights itself. Some medical authorities estimate that eighty-five per cent of the illnesses in our pressurized society are psychosomatic.

Undoubtedly there was an element of this dimension in our Lord's healings, but some were clearly outside this category. Take, for instance, the healings of leprosy. Obviously these did not have a psychosomatic base. Lepers who were made well experienced the direct power of God. Then there are the clear cases of healing of congenital disease, such as the man born blind (Jn 9). Since this man was born with his blindness, it could obviously not be accounted for on a psychosomatic basis, and for the same reasons neither could his receiving his sight.

This case illustrates the fallacy of another notion common among modern thinkers. We must remember, it is said, that people in ancient times were exceedingly ignorant, gullible and superstitious. They thought many things were miracles that we now know, with the benefit of modern science, were not miracles at all, but simply phenomena which people didn't understand. For instance, if we were to fly a modern jet over a primitive tribe today, they would probably fall to the ground in worship of this "silver bird god" of the sky. They would think that the sight they observed was a miraculous phenomenon. We, however, know that the plane is simply a result of the applied principles of aerodynamics, and we realize there is nothing miraculous about it at all.

The problem with this thesis, which sounds so plausible at first, is that many of the miracles are not of this order. In the case of the blind man, the people observed that since the beginning of time it had not been known for a man born blind to receive his sight. And we have no more *natural* explanation of this miracle now than was available then. And who, today, has any more explanation, in a natural sense, of our Lord's resurrection from the dead than was available when it happened? No one! We simply cannot get away from the supernatural aspects of the biblical record.

Not in Conflict with Natural Law

It is important to note, however, that miracles are not in conflict with any natural law. Rather, as J. N. Hawthorne puts it, "Miracles are *unusual* events caused by God. The laws of nature are generalizations about ordinary events caused by him."[1]

There are two views among thinking Christians as to the relationship of miracles to natural law. Some suggest that miracles employ a "higher" natural law, which at present is unknown to us. It is quite obvious that despite all of the impressive discoveries of modern science, we are still standing on the seashore of an ocean of ignorance. When we have increased our knowledge sufficiently, this thesis says, we will realize that the things we today thought were miracles were merely the working out of the higher laws of the universe, of which we were not aware at the time.

But a *law*, in the modern scientific sense, is that which is regular and acts uniformly. To say that a miracle is the result of a higher *law*, then, is to use the term in a way that is different from its customary usage and meaning.

An Act of Creation

On the other hand, there are those Christian thinkers who view miracles as an act of creation—a sovereign, transcendent act of God's supernatural power. It would seem that this is the more appropriate view.

Biblical miracles, in contrast to miracle stories in pagan literature and those of other religions, were never capricious or fantastic. They were not scattered helter-skelter through the record without rhyme or reason. There was always clear order and purpose to them. They cluster around three periods of biblical history: the exodus, the prophets who led Israel, and the time of Christ and the early church. They always had as their purpose to confirm faith by authenticating the message and the messenger, or to demonstrate God's love by relieving suffering. They were never performed as entertainment, as a magician puts on a show for his patrons.

Miracles were never performed for personal prestige or to gain money or power. Our Lord was tempted by the devil in the wilderness to use his miracle power in just this way, but he steadfastly refused. As an evidence of the truth of the Christian message, however, our Lord referred to great miracles.

In answer to the direct request of the Jews to tell them plainly if he was the Messiah, he said, "I did tell you, but you do not believe. The miracles I do in my Father's name speak for me" (Jn 10:25). Again he says that if they had any hesitation in believing his claims they should believe him "on the evidence of the miracles themselves" (14:11).

God confirmed the message of the apostles in the fledgling church with signs and wonders.

Why Not Now?

People often say, "If God performed miracles *then,* why does he not do them *now?* If I saw a miracle I could believe!" This question was answered in our Lord's time. A rich man who was in the torment of hell lifted up his eyes and pleaded with Abraham that someone should warn his five brothers lest they too should come into the awful place. He was told that his brothers had the Scriptures. But the rich man protested that if one should rise from the dead, they would be shaken by the miracle and would take heed. The reply given applies as much today as then: "If they do not listen to Moses and the Prophets," Abraham said, "they will not be convinced even if someone rises from the dead" (Lk 16:31). And so it is today. Many have made a rationalistic presupposition which rules out the very possibility of miracles. Since they know miracles are impossible, no amount of evidence would ever persuade them one had taken place. There would always be an alternate naturalistic explanation for them to advance.

We Have Reliable Records

Miracles are not necessary for us today because we already have reliable records of those miracles which have occurred. As Ramm observes, "If miracles are capable of sensory perception, they can be made matters of testimony. If they are adequately testified to, then the recorded testimony has the same validity for evidence as the experience of beholding the event."[2]

Every court in the world operates on the basis of reliable testimony by word of mouth or in writing. "If the raising of Lazarus was actually witnessed by John and recorded faithfully by him when still in soundness of faculties and memory, for purposes of evidence it is the same as if we were there and saw it."[3] Ramm then lists reasons we may know that the miracles have adequate and reliable testimony. We summarize:

■ *First, many miracles were done in public.* They were not performed in secret before only one or two people, who announced them to the world. There was every opportunity to investigate the miracles on the spot. It is very impressive that the opponents of Jesus never denied the fact of the miracles he performed. They either attributed them to the power of Satan or else tried to suppress the evidence, as with the raising of Lazarus from the dead. They said, in effect, "Let's kill him before the people realize what is happening and the whole world goes after him!"

■ *Second, some miracles were performed before unbelievers.* It is significant that the miracles claimed by cults and offbeat groups never seem to happen when the skeptic is present to observe. It was not so with Jesus.

■ *Third, the miracles of Jesus were performed over a period of time and involved a great variety of powers.* He had power over nature, as when he turned the water to wine; he had power over disease, as when he healed the lepers and the blind; he had power over demons, as was shown by his casting them out; he had supernatural powers of knowledge, as in his knowing that Nathanael was under a fig tree; he demonstrated his power of creation when he fed 5,000 people from a few loaves and fish; and he exhibited power over death itself in the raising of Lazarus and others.

■ *Fourth, we have the testimony of the cured.* As noted earlier, we have it from those, like Lazarus, whose healings could not have been psychosomatic or a result of inaccurate diagnosis.

■ *Fifth, we cannot discount the gospel miracles because of the extravagant claim of pagan miracles.*

> Miracles are believed in non-Christian religions because the religion is already believed, but in the biblical religion, miracles are part of the means of establishing the true religion. This distinction is of immense importance. Israel was brought into existence by a series of miracles, the Law was given surrounded by supernatural wonders, and many of the prophets were identified as God's spokesmen by their power to perform miracles. Jesus came not only preaching but performing miracles, and the apostles from time to time worked wonders. It was the miracle authenticating the religion at every point.[4]

As C. S. Lewis wrote, "All the essentials of Hinduism would, I think, remain unimpaired if you subtracted the miraculous, and the same is almost true of Muhammedanism, but you cannot do that with Christianity. It is precisely the story of a great miracle. A naturalistic Christianity leaves out all that is specifically Christian."[5]

Pagan Miracles

Miracles recorded outside the Bible do not display the same order, dignity and motive as those in Scripture. But what is more important, they do not have the same solid authentication as the biblical miracles. We have discussed at some length the historical reliability of Bible records. Similar investigations into pagan records of miracles would soon show there is no basis for comparison.

The same could be said of many so-called miracles and alleged healings of our own time. They do not stand the full weight of investigation. But to take some ancient pagan miracle, or a contemporary claim, and to show their great improbability is not fair to biblical miracles. The fact that some miracles are counterfeits is no proof that *all* are spurious, any more than the discovery of some counterfeit currency would prove all currency spurious.

Exaggerated Reporting

Some attempts have been made to explain miracles on the basis of exaggerated reporting. It has been demonstrated that people are notoriously inaccurate in reporting events and impressions. Playing the simple parlor game of Rumor is enough to confirm this fact. In the light of this tendency, we are told, it is obvious that the reliability of a human being as an observer may be severely questioned. Consequently, we can discount the gospel accounts of miracles as the mistaken observations of inaccurate and imaginative observers.

It may be answered that despite this tendency, law courts have not ceased functioning, and eyewitnesses are still considered able to provide highly useful information. And though there may be some question about such details of an accident as the time, speed of the cars, etc., the accident cannot be said not to have happened because of discrepancies in witnesses' stories. As Ramm observes, the smashed cars and the injured people are irrefutable evidence on which all agreed.[6]

We must be careful to see the limitations of arguments such as the unreliability of witnesses. It will help us greatly to see that some of these arguments, pressed to their outer limits, refute the very assertions they set out to make. For instance, those conducting the experiments to establish the unreliability of human witnesses must assume their own reliability or they will have to throw out their own conclusions as being the result of human observation, which is unreliable!

Believers Can't Be Objective

Another erroneous idea, sometimes advanced, is that the miracle stories must be discarded because they are told by believing disciples and are therefore not objective. But the disciples were the ones on the scene who saw the miracles. The fact that they were disciples is neither here nor there. The question is, Did they tell the truth? As we have seen, eyewitness testimony is the best we can get, and most of the disciples faced the test of death as the test of their veracity.

We would not today, in a court of law, say that in order to guarantee objectivity on the part of witnesses, we will listen only to those who were not at the scene of an accident and had nothing to do with it. Nor would we say we would not take testimony from eyewitnesses, including the victims, because they would be prejudiced. The crucial question in each case is truthfulness, not proximity or relationship to the events.

The Question Is Philosophical

We have seen that the question of whether miracles are possible is not scientific, but philosophical. Science can only say miracles do not occur in the ordinary course of nature. Science cannot forbid miracles because natural laws do not cause, and therefore cannot forbid, anything. They are merely descriptions of what happens. The Christian embraces the concept of natural law. "It is essential to the theistic doctrine of miracles that nature be uniform in her daily routine. If nature were utterly spontaneous, miracles would be as impossible of detection as it would be to establish a natural law."[7]

It is "scientism," rather than science, which says miracles cannot happen. The scientist, like anyone else, can only ask, "Are the records of miracles historically reliable?"

Further, we have seen the miracles in the Bible are an inherent part of God's communication to us—not a mere appendage of little significance. We have seen that the whole question ultimately depends on the existence of God. Settle that question and miracles cease to be a problem. The very uniformity against which a miracle stands in stark contrast depends on an omnipotent author of natural law, who is also capable of transcending it to accomplish his sovereign ends.

For Individual or Group Study

1. Think back. When you have read of Christ's miracles in the Gospels, what reactions have you had?

2. What do we mean by *natural law* or the *laws of nature* (p. 102)?

3. Is God ruled by the laws of nature? Explain.

4. What is the relationship between the laws of nature and miracles (pp. 102-5)?

5. The author reports that some health authorities believe eighty-five per cent of illness is psychosomatic (pp. 103-4). Do you believe Christ healed only psychosomatic illnesses when he was on earth? Explain.

6. What two purposes did biblical miracles fulfill (pp. 105-6)?

7. The chapter contends that having the completed revelation of God in the Bible, we no longer need new miracles performed for our own science-oriented generation (p. 107). Do you agree with this? Why or why not?

8. Do you believe having the Bible to read fulfills the second purpose of miracles, "to demonstrate God's love by relieving suffering"? Why or why not?

9. Besides miracles, in what ways does God use his people to accomplish God's purposes of confirming faith and demonstrating God's love by relieving suffering?

10. How can you tell the difference between biblical miracles from "pagan" miracles (pp. 108-9)?

11. What reasons have been offered for dismissing the disciples' testimony concerning the miracles Christ performed (pp. 109-11)?

12. How valid do you think these criticisms are?

13. Many times when a person expresses doubts about miracles or prophecy, the person has a deeper problem underneath. How can you get to the root cause of the disbelief?

14. Take time now to add any new insights to your list of reasons for putting

your hope in God through Christ Jesus. Space is provided following page 173.

For Further Reading

Fischer, Robert. *God Did It But How?: Relationships between the Bible and Science.* La Mirada, Calif.: California Media, 1981.
Lewis, C. S. *Miracles.* New York: Macmillan, 1978.

9
Do Science and Scripture Agree?

IF EVER THERE WAS A QUESTION WHICH HAS GENERATED MORE HEAT than light, it is: "Do science and Scripture agree?" Some say there is conflict. Most of the apparent conflict stems from making the Bible say things it really does not say and from scientism, a philosophic interpretation of scientific facts. These interpretations are distinct from the facts themselves.

To the question, "Have some scientists and some Christians disagreed?" the answer would have to be a resounding yes! We need only recall the church's persecution of Galileo, the Scopes trial of 1925 or the confrontation a century ago between Wilberforce and Huxley, to know this is the case.

Well-Meaning Christians
Part of the problem, as we have indicated, stems from some well-

meaning but misguided Christians who make the Bible say what it does not say. One classic and harmful example is the Bible chronology calculated by Bishop James Ussher (1581-1656), a contemporary of Shakespeare. He worked out a series of dates from the genealogies in the Bible and concluded that the world was created in 4004 B.C.

It is thought by many non-Christians, including the famous Lord Bertrand Russell, that Christians actually believe creation occurred in 4004 B.C. Some time ago I was visiting a non-Christian student at a Midwestern state university campus. He picked up a true-false exam in a course on Western Civilization. One question read, "According to the Bible, the world was created in 4004 B.C."

"I suppose your instructor wants you to mark this question true," I said.

"That's right," the student replied.

"Interesting," I mused. Pulling an Oxford edition of the Bible from my pocket, I said, "I wonder if you could show me where the Bible says that."

The student was puzzled that he couldn't find the date on the first page of Genesis. Trying to be helpful, a Christian student who was with me volunteered, "It's on page 3."

It was news to both of them that Bishop Ussher's dates, which appear in some English Bibles, are not part of the original text.

On the other hand, some scientists are given to making statements beyond the facts. These statements are philosophic interpretations of data which do not carry the same weight of authority as the data. Unfortunately, the facts and the interpretations are seldom distinguished in the minds of listeners.

When a Scientist Speaks

When a scientist speaks on *any* subject, he is likely to be believed. He may be speaking outside his field, but the same respect that should rightfully be given to his statements from within his field are almost unconsciously transferred to *everything* he says. For instance, Carl Sagan, well-known author and professor of astronomy at Cornell University, illustrates this crossover from science to "scientism." *U.S. News and World Report* interviewed him on the subject of science and religion! Science is his field; religion certainly is not! However, he makes bold religious pronouncements: "The cosmos is all that is or ever was or ever will be;" "Whatever significance we humans have is that which we make ourselves"; and "If we must worship a power greater than ourselves, does it not make sense to worship the sun and the stars?" This raises the question as to why we would worship nature if it is, as he states, "the result of blind chance and part of a pointless process"?[1]

Honest Differences

If we limit ourselves to what the Bible actually says and to what the scientific facts actually are, we shrink the area of controversy enormously. It should be noted here that there may be honest differences of opinion among equally orthodox and committed Christians as to what the Bible means in some instances. Consider the meaning of *day* in Genesis 1. We must be slow to condemn as a heretic someone whose interpretation of a particular passage may differ from ours. As long as one agrees that what the Bible teaches is authoritative, he is within the bounds of orthodoxy.

Faith Is Suspect

Another area in which conflict has arisen is on the question of whether those things which cannot be verified by the scientific method are valid and real. Some people consciously, and others unconsciously, assume that if a statement cannot be proved in a laboratory by the methods of natural science, it is untrustworthy and cannot be accepted as reliable. The findings of science are considered to be objective and therefore real; statements that must be accepted by faith are looked on as suspect. E. C. Wilson, widely respected astronomer, illustrates this position in his book *On Human Nature*. He states, "The final decisive edge enjoyed by scientific naturalism will come from its capacity to explain traditional religion, its chief competitor [sic], as a wholly material phenomenon."[2]

But there are ways and means other than the laboratory to acquire real and genuine knowledge. Consider the process of falling in love. This surely is not done in a laboratory, with a battery of instruments, but anyone who has ever experienced it would be the last to admit that his knowledge of love is uncertain or unreal. We have seen earlier that the scientific method is valid only for those realities which are measurable in physical terms. God is a different kind of reality from the world of nature which science examines. God does not await someone's empirical investigation; he is a personal being who has revealed himself in love and can be known in personal presence.

Scientific Methods

Faith is no detriment to the apprehension of reality. In fact, science itself rests on presuppositions which must be accepted by faith before research is possible. One such assumption is that the universe is orderly, that it operates according to a pattern, and that therefore one can predict its behavior.

It should be observed here that the scientific method, as we know it today, began in the sixteenth century among people who were Christians. Breaking with the Greek polytheistic concepts which viewed the universe as capricious and irregular, and therefore not capable of systematic study, they reasoned that the universe must be orderly and worthy of investigation because it was the work of an intelligent Creator. In pursuing scientific research, they were convinced they were thinking God's thoughts after him.

Another unprovable presupposition that must be accepted by

faith is the reliability of our sense perceptions. One must believe that our senses are trustworthy enough to get a true picture of the universe and enable us to understand its orderliness.

Science Is Only One Way to Truth

Christians, then, believe that science is one avenue to the discovery of truth about physical things, but that there are other non-material realities and other means of attaining truth. A Christian exercises faith and has presuppositions, as does a scientist, and in this he sees nothing incompatible with reason or intelligence. It is apparent that there are many Christians who are scientists. They do not consider themselves intellectual schizophrenics, but rather view themselves as following in the footsteps of the Christian founders of modern science.

It should further be recognized that science is incapable of making value judgments about the things it measures. Many people on the frontiers of science are realizing that there is nothing inherent in science to guide them in the application of the discoveries they make. There is nothing in science itself which will determine whether nuclear energy will be used to destroy cities or destroy cancer. This is a judgment outside the scientific method to determine.

Further, science can tell us how something works but not *why* it works that way. Whether there is any purpose in the universe can never be answered for us by science. As one writer put it, "Science can give us the 'know-how,' but it cannot give us the 'know-why.' "[3]

We are dependent on revelation for many kinds of information, the absence of which leaves us with a quite incomplete picture. The Bible does not purport to tell us the *how* of many things, but it clearly gives us the *why.*

This is not to say that when the Scriptures refer to matters of science and history they are inaccurate, but rather to point out that the Scriptures have a different focus of attention.

Is God Necessary?

Humility, then, is a valuable virtue for a non-Christian scientist and for a Christian, be he scientist or not. Incalculable harm has been done by the use of argument by ridicule. A sarcastic remark is always good for a long, loud laugh from some of the faithful, but invariably it loses the thoughtful person, wavering in his conviction, and the timid unbeliever making his first tentative investigation.

Some have erroneously thought that God was necessary to explain areas of life and existence for which at the moment there was no other explanation. Unbelieving scientists seize on this concept to point out that these gaps are narrowing. "Give us enough time," they say, "and humans will be able to explain how everything in the universe works."

Those who adopt this point of view forget that God is not only Creator, but also sustainer. "He is before all things, and in him all things hold together" (Col 1:17). The universe would fall apart without his sustaining power. Even if people understand everything, they will still need God. Knowing how the universe is sustained is not the same thing as sustaining it.

For instance, there are striking new advances today in the field of genetic engineering. DNA, the key chemical that manages heredity, has been produced in a laboratory, and scientists are projecting undreamed-of possibilities. What does all this mean to the Christian? Will God somehow be torn from his throne? In fact, the exact opposite is the case. The advances of science have only emphasized that life did not come by blind chance, but by an intelligent mind, as the result of prodigious thought and work under the most rigidly controlled conditions. Recent discoveries would argue for theism rather than the opposite. And we still must account for the elements scientists used to produce life. Where did they come

from? Could they have merely evolved? The most logical explanation is that God created those elements. If humans can, in fact,
think God's thoughts after him, it should follow that humans will
mimic God's processes—but they have not thereby become God.

Today the question of evolution can create a veritable storm of
conflict. The very word *evolution* starts the adrenal glands working
overtime. Part of the tension arises from casting the problem into
black-and-white terms. Many think that either a person believes in
total fiat creation or he is an agnostic or atheistic evolutionist.

Whenever the term *evolution* is used, however, we should define
what we mean and ask others, when they use it, to define precisely
what they mean by it. At the risk of oversimplification, we will
consider three general views of evolution.

Three Views of Evolution

■ The first we may call *evolutionism.* Those who hold this world
view believe that the universe has been evolving forever on the
basis of natural processes, mutation and natural selection.

■ Second, there is the view called *microevolution* describing a
continued process of change or development within a species. G.
A. Kerkut, an evolutionist, described it as "many living animals
observed over the course of time which undergo change so that
new [varieties] are formed."[4] These changes may be chromosome
changes, gene mutations or hybridization to produce new varieties.
But the changes have always been seen to remain within their
species. As has been said, "A horse is still a horse." Or, "No protozoa to a man."

To illustrate, if a mutation takes place within the genes of the
earthworm, providing it with increased dexterity against predatory
blackbirds, the carriers of this mutation will fare better in the
earthworm's struggle for survival. This mutation will improve the
worm—but strictly as a worm. This is microevolution within a species.

In connection with this, it's important to understand that a species is one of seven classifications of all living plants and animals listed by Swedish naturalist Carolus Linnaeus. The groups are: (1) kingdom; (2) phylum; (3) class; (4) order; (5) family; (6) genus; and (7) species. The kingdom is the largest group and the species is the smallest. Members of a species have a high degree of similarity among themselves and generally interbreed only with themselves.

Microevolution will allow for creation of new species, but not the development of one species to a higher classification. Most contemporary evangelical scholars would agree that this kind of evolution takes place.

But we may logically ask if the Genesis word *kind* is the same as *species?* Dr. Kenneth Kantzer, author and theologian, states this word is not. It is "simply 'kind' in a most general way, and could apply to anything from a Linnean phylum to a Linnean species. It is even pressing too much into the phrase 'after its kind' to interpret it to mean that God individually created each 'kind' by a separate act . . . [but] each kind reproduces offspring like itself."[5]

■ The third view is *macroevolution*, also called *megaevolution*, which requires the transfer of genetic information to a higher, more complex classification, the boundaries being crossed by mutation and natural selection.

A. E. Wilder-Smith, professor of pharmacology, points out that these factors along with chance "cannot provide the information necessary to build legs onto a fish, thus permitting it to leave the water and to walk on land. Paleontology, for example, knows of no missing links (transitional forms) between whales and land mammals that have ever been established. Intermediate links of this sort would probably have been incapable of living. . . . For over 120 years geology has been searching for these links in vain."[6] Actually, it is erroneous to speak of *the* missing link. There are thousands of missing links!

Animal Ancestors?

When Christians consider these various views of evolution and the origins of human beings, they must hold to two non-negotiables: God supernaturally and deliberately created the heavens and the earth (Gen 1:1), and God supernaturally and deliberately created the first man and the first woman (1:27). We do not shrink from these two limits. The Genesis account tells us God made Adam and then made Eve from Adam's side, both "made in God's image." When God breathed into Adam the breath of life, that set him apart from anything else God had made. This was a first! It also rules out the possibility suggested by some that people evolved from any animal ancestor.

It is helpful to read the New Testament references that confirm Adam and Eve as historic (Rom 5:12, 14; 1 Cor 15:22, 45; 2 Cor 11:3; 1 Tim 2:13- 14; 1 Jn 3:12; Jude 11). A careful understanding of these passages leaves no room for the possibility that the Genesis story is an allegory. Francis Schaeffer states, "God gave us religious truths in a book of history and a book that touches on the cosmos as well. What sense does it make for God to give us true religious truths and at the same time place them in a book that is wrong when it touches history and the cosmos?"[7]

What about the Age of the Earth?

From the biblical record, some Christians assume the earth must have been created not too many thousands of years before the birth of Christ. Yet, they believe from science that the earth must be millions or billions of years old and feel squeamish about it. The question is: "Can we date the earth from the biblical records?"

Let's look at the use of the Hebrew word *day*. Can it mean periods of time rather than a single twenty-four-hour day? In Genesis 5:2 the word is used to describe the creation of Adam and Eve on the sixth day. And notice Adam's activities on the sixth day: He named all the animals, did not find a "suitable helper," and Eve was created—all on the sixth day! It seems that even with the most literal interpretation of this day, the sixth day was a longer period of time.

The use of the same word in other passages shows the Lord's concept of day is not so confined. For instance, "A thousand years in your sight are like a day that has just gone by" (Ps 90:4) and "With the Lord a day is like a thousand years" (2 Pet 3:8). Theologian Davis Young notes that "the language of Genesis 1 (for example, the development of vegetation on day three) strongly implies the processes of natural growth and development, initiated by the fiat of God's word ('Let the earth produce grass')."

It should be noted that some highly intelligent evangelical scholars interpret the Genesis account as describing twenty-four-hour days, a "grown-up" universe, trees with rings, etc., and we need to consider their arguments. However, Young speaks to this: "The Christian geologist need not assume that all geological features were created with an appearance of age. He may assume that rocks, mountains, and other geological features of the six days of creation were formed through processes analogous with those of the present. And he has the right to use evidence contained in those rocks to reconstruct the past by analogy with the present. This also helps us avoid the problem of why God should have created a rock deposit that looked as if it had been formed by glacial action but really had not."[8]

In summary, Kantzer states, "As biblical students, therefore, we must remain agnostic about the age of the earth. We have no biblical warrant for ruling out the validity of the commonly accepted geological timetable. Let scientists battle it out on the basis of the scientific evidence, but we should not bolster weak scientific positions with misinterpretations of the Bible conjured up for that purpose. God rarely sees fit merely to gratify our curiosity."[9] In matters where God chooses to be silent, we should likewise choose to remain silent.

A Constantly Moving Train

Scientific theory is a matter of the highest degree of probability based on the data available. There are no absolutes in it. Furthermore, science is a train that is constantly moving. Yesterday's generalization is today's discarded hypothesis. This is one reason for being somewhat tentative about accepting any form of evolutionary theory as the final explanation of biology. It is also why it is dangerous to try to prove the Bible by science. If the Bible becomes wedded to today's scientific theories, what will happen to it when science, ten years from now, has shifted?

Theologian W. A. Criswell cites: "In 1861 . . . the French Academy of Science published a little brochure in which they stated fifty-one scientific facts that controverted the Word of God. Today there is not a scientist in the world who believes a single one of those fifty-one so-called scientific facts that in 1861 were published as controverting the Word of God. Not a one!"[10]

Thoughtful evolutionists concede that the matter is not an open-and-shut case, but they feel the theory must be accepted despite some seeming contradictions and unexplained factors.

The following is of such interest that I quote it at length to illustrate this point. After discussing how pathetically theology students at Cambridge, in a former century, accepted dogma and teachings they did not fully understand or personally investigate, G. A. Kerkut, an evolutionist, points out that many present-day undergraduates have succumbed to the same unthinking tendencies in their studies in general, and in accepting evolution in biology in particular. He writes:

> For some years now I have tutored undergraduates on various aspects of biology. It is quite common, during the course of conversation, to ask the student if he knows the evidence for evolution. This usually evokes a faintly superior smile. . . . "Well, sir, there is the evidence from paleontology, comparative anatomy, embryology, systematics and geographical distribu-

tions," the student would say in a nursery-rhyme jargon. . . .

"Do you think that the evolutionary theory is the best explanation yet advanced to explain animal interrelationships?" I would ask.

"Why, of course, sir," would be the reply. "There is nothing else, except for the religious explanation held by some fundamentalist Christians, and I gather, sir, that these views are no longer held by the more up-to-date churchmen."

"So you believe in evolution because there is no other theory?"

"Oh, no, sir, I believe in it because of the evidence I just mentioned."

"Have you read any book on the evidence for evolution?" I would ask.

"Yes, sir." And here he would mention the names of authors of a popular school textbook. "And of course, sir, there is that book by Darwin, *The Origin of Species.*"

"Have you read this book?" I would ask.

"Well, not all through, sir."

"The first fifty pages?"

"Yes, sir, about that much; maybe a bit less."

"I see. And that has given you your firm understanding of evolution?"

"Yes, sir."

"Well, now, if you really understand an argument you will be able to indicate to me not only the points in favor of the argument, but also the most telling points against it."

"I suppose so, sir."

"Good. Please tell me, then, some of the evidence against the theory of evolution."

"But there isn't any, sir."

Here the conversation would take on a more strained atmosphere. The student would look at me as if I were playing a very unfair game. He would take it rather badly when I suggested that he was not being very scientific in his outlook if he swallowed the latest scientific dogma and, when questioned, just repeated parrot-fashion the views of the current Archbishop of Evolution. In fact he would be behaving like certain of those religious students he affected to despise. He would be taking on faith what he could not intellectually understand and, when questioned, would appeal to authority of a "good book," which in this case was *The Origin of Species*. (It is interesting to note that many of these widely quoted books are read by title only. Three of such that come to mind are the Bible, *The Origin of Species*, and *Das Kapital*.)

I would suggest that the student should go away and read the evidence for and against evolution and present it as an essay. A week would pass and the same student would appear armed with an essay on the evidence for evolution. The essay would usually be well done, since the student might have realized that I should be rough to convince. When the essay had been read and the question concerning the evidence against evolution came up, the student would give a rather pained smile. "Well, sir, I looked up various books but could not find anything in the scientific books against evolution. I did not think you would want a religious argument."

"No, you were quite correct. I want a scientific argument against evolution."

"Well, sir, there does not seem to be one, and that in itself is a piece of evidence in favor of the evolutionary theory."

I would then indicate to him that the theory of evolution was of considerable antiquity, and would mention that he might have looked at the book by Radi, *The History of Biological Theories*. Having made sure the student had noted the book down for future reference I would proceed as follows:

Before one can decide that the theory of evolution is the best explanation of the present-day range of forms of living material, one should examine all the implications that such a theory may hold. Too often the theory is applied to, say, the development of the horse, and then, because it is held to be applicable there, it is extended to the rest of the animal kingdom with little or no further evidence.

There are, however, seven basic assumptions that are often not mentioned during discussions of evolution. Many evolutionists ignore the first six assumptions and consider only the seventh.

The first assumption is that nonliving things gave rise to living material, i.e., that spontaneous generation occurred.

The second assumption is that spontaneous generation occurred only once.

The third . . . is that viruses, bacteria, plants, and animals are all interrelated.

The fourth . . . is that the protozoa gave rise to the metazoa.

The fifth . . . is that the various invertebrate phyla are interrelated.

The sixth . . . is that the invertebrates gave rise to the vertebrates.

The seventh . . . is that the vertebrates and fish gave rise to the amphibia, the amphibia to the reptiles, and the reptiles to the birds and mammals. Sometimes this is expressed in other words, i.e., that the modern amphibia and reptiles had a common ancestral stock and so on.

For the initial purposes of this discussion on evolution I shall consider that the supporters of the theory of evolution hold that all these seven assumptions are valid, and that these assumptions form the general theory of evolution.

The first point that I should like to make is that *the seven assumptions by their nature are not capable of experimental verification* [italics mine]. They assume that a certain series of events has occurred in the past. Thus, though it may be possible to mimic some of these events under present-day conditions, this does not mean that these events must therefore have taken place in the past. All that it shows is that it is *possible* for such a change to take place. Thus, to change a present-day reptile into a mammal, though of great interest, would not show the way in which the mammals *did* arise. Unfortunately, we cannot bring about even this change; instead we have to depend upon limited circumstantial evidence for our assumptions.[11]

Here we must remember that it is useless to get into a discussion of evolution with a non-Christian. Rather, when the subject comes up, I first ask the evolutionist whether he is concluding from his position that there is no God and that everything happened by chance, or whether he concedes God is the initiator of life. If he accepts, the latter, I confront him directly with Jesus Christ. He is the real issue in salvation, not one's view of evolution. When the issue of Christ is settled, other less important ones settle themselves in due course.

Two extremes must be avoided. First is the assumption that evolution has been proved without doubt and that anyone with a brain in his head must accept it. The second is the notion that evolution is "only a theory," with little evidence for it.

We reiterate that the so-called conflicts of science and the Bible are often conflicts between interpretations of the facts.

The presupposition one brings to the facts, rather than the facts themselves, determines one's conclusion. For instance, one might be told that his wife was seen riding around town with another man. Knowing his wife, he draws a different conclusion from this fact than does the town gossip. The different conclusions result, not from different facts, but from different presuppositions brought to the fact.

In everything we read and in everything we hear we must ask, "What is this person's presupposition?" so that we may interpret conclusions in this light. There is no such thing as total objectivity.

The Christian can never forget that God can act in miraculous ways and in the past he often chose to. The Bible discloses that he was involved in his original creation and continues in a wise and purposeful relationship with it. While there are problems for which there is as yet no explanation, there is no fundamental conflict between science and Scripture.

For Individual or Group Study

1. What can happen when authorities, such as Bible scholars or scientists, make assumptions beyond the scope of their discipline (pp. 113-15)?

2. What would you say is the difference between *science* and *scientism?*
What are some examples?

3. How have well-meaning Jews or Christians "added to the Word of God"?

4. Why do we limit the controversy between science and Scripture by "sticking to the facts" (p. 115)?
What "facts" are valid to discuss?

5. Paul Little cautions against two extremes Christians should avoid in viewing evolution: (1) that evolution has been proven without a doubt; (2) that evolution is only a theory with little evidence behind it (p. 127). How has evolution been presented to you in the past in secular and Christian settings?

6. After reading this chapter, how do you view evolution and creationism?

7. The author suggests that we should "first ask the evolutionist whether he is concluding from his position that there is no God and that everything happened by chance, or whether he concedes God is the initiator of life" (p. 127). Think about a friend who believes in evolution. How would you steer the conversation away from a scientific debate to a discussion of Christ and his claims?

8. On page 127 the author says, "The presupposition one brings to the facts, rather than the facts themselves, determines one's conclusion." Can you think of ways you have assumed that science must be "wrong" out of fear that it contradicts Scripture? If so, what are they?
What do you think now?

9. If you have been skeptical about science for fear it contradicted what a Christian should believe, what are some ways you could open up to science without compromising your Christ-centered presuppositions.

10. Take time now to add any new insights to your list of reasons for putting your hope in God through Christ Jesus. Space is provided following page 173.

For Further Reading

Hummel, Charles E. *The Galileo Connection.* Downers Grove, Ill.: InterVarsity Press, 1986.

Ratzsch, Del. *Philosophy of Science: The Natural Sciences in Christian Perspective.* Downers Grove, Ill.: InterVarsity Press, 1986.

MacKay, Donald. *The Clockwork Image.* Downers Grove, Ill.: InterVarsity Press; Leicester, England: Inter-Varsity Press, 1974.

Van Till, Howard, Young, Davis, and Menninga, Clarence. *Science Held Hostage.* Downers Grove, Ill.: InterVarsity Press, 1988.

10
Why Does God Allow Suffering and Evil?

●●●●●●●●●●●

WHY GOD ALLOWS SUFFERING AND EVIL IS ONE OF THE MOST pressing questions of our time. More pressing than the question of miracles or science and the Bible is the poignant problem of why innocent people suffer, why babies are born blind or why a promising life is snuffed out as it is on the rise. Why are there wars in which thousands of innocent people are killed, children are burned beyond recognition and many are maimed for life?

In the classic statement of the problem: either God is all-powerful but not all-good, and therefore doesn't stop evil; or he is all-good but unable to stop evil, in which case he is not all-powerful.

The general tendency is to blame God for evil and suffering and to pass on all responsibility for it to him.

No Easy Answers

This profound question is not one to be treated lightly or in doctrinaire fashion. We must never forget that when God created Adam and Eve, he created them perfect. They were not created evil. Adam and Eve did, however, as human beings, have ability to obey or disobey God. Had they obeyed God there would never have been a problem. They would have lived an unending life of blissful fellowship with God and enjoyment of him and his creation. This is what God intended for them when he created them. In fact, however, they rebelled against God—and every one of us from that time until now has ratified that rebellion. "Therefore, just as sin entered the world through one man, and death through sin, and in this way death came to all men, because all sinned" (Rom 5:12). We must remember that *people* are responsible for sin—not God.

But many ask, "Why didn't God make us so we couldn't sin?" To be sure, he could have, but let's remember that if he had done so we would no longer be human beings, we would be machines. How would you like to be married to a mechanical doll? Every morning and every night you could pull the string and get the beautiful words, "I love you." But who would want that? There would never be any love, either. Love is voluntary. God could have made us like robots, but we would have ceased to be human. God apparently thought it worth the risk of creating us as we are. In any case he did it and we must face the realities.

God Could Stamp Out Evil!

Jeremiah reminds us, "Because of the LORD's great love we are not consumed, for his compassions never fail" (Lam 3:22). A time is coming when he will stamp out evil in the world. The devil and all his works will come under eternal judgment. In the meantime, God's unchanging love and grace prevail and his marvelous offer of mercy and pardon is still open to everyone.

If God were to stamp out evil today, he would do a complete job.

We want him to stop war but stay remote from us. If God were to remove evil from the universe, his action would be complete and would have to include our lies and personal impurities, our lack of love and our failure to do good. Suppose God were to decree that tonight all evil would be removed from the universe—who of us would still be here after midnight?

What God Has Done about the Evil

He has done the most dramatic, costly and effective thing possible by giving his Son to die for evil human beings. It is possible for people to escape God's inevitable judgment on sin and evil. It is also possible to have its power broken by entering into a personal relationship with the Lord Jesus Christ. The ultimate answer to the problem of evil, at the personal level, is found in the sacrificial death of Jesus Christ.

To speculate about the origin of evil is endless. No one has the full answer. It belongs in the category of "the secret things [that] belong to the LORD our God" (Deut 29:29).

Part of our problem arises from our limited definition of the word *good* and our applying this term to God. Hugh Evan Hopkins observes:

In his famous essay on nature, John Stuart Mill clearly sets out the problem with which thinkers all through history have wrestled: If the law of all creation were justice and the Creator omnipotent, then in whatever amount suffering and happiness might be dispensed to the world, each person's share would be exactly proportioned to that person's good or evil deeds. No human being would have a worse lot than another without worse deserts; accident or favoritism would have no part in such a world, but every human life would be playing out a drama constructed like a perfect moral tale. Not even on the most distorted and contracted theory of good which ever was framed by religious or philosophical fanaticism can the government of

134 _____Know Why You Believe

nature be made to resemble the work of a being at once both good and omnipotent.[1]

The problem arises largely from the belief that a good God would reward each man according to his deserts and that an *almighty* God would have no difficulty in carrying this out. The fact that rewards and punishments, in the way of happiness and discomfort, appear to be haphazardly distributed in this life drives many to question either the goodness of God or his power.[2]

Exact-Reward Concept

But would God be good if he were to deal with each person exactly according to his behavior? Consider what this would mean in your own life! The whole of the gospel as previewed in the Old Testament and broadcast in stereo-television in the New Testament is that God's goodness consists not only in his justice but also in his love, mercy and kindness. How thankful we and all people should be that "he does not treat us as our sins deserve or repay us according to our iniquities. For as high as the heavens are above the earth, so great is his love for those who fear him" (Ps 103:10-11).

Such a concept of the goodness of God is also based on the faulty assumption that happiness is the greatest good in life. Happiness is usually thought of in terms of comfort. True, genuine, deep-seated happiness, however, is something much more profound than the ephemeral, fleeting enjoyment of the moment. And true happiness is not precluded by suffering. Sometimes, in his infinite wisdom, God knows that there are things to be accomplished in our character that can be brought only through suffering. To shield us from this suffering would be to rob us of a greater good. The apostle Peter refers to this when he says, "And the God of all grace, who called you to his eternal glory in Christ, after you have suffered a little while, will himself restore you and make you strong, firm and steadfast" (1 Pet 5:10).

To see the logical consequence of Mill's *exact reward* concept of God in his dealings with us, we need only turn to Hinduism. The law of Karma says that all of the actions of life today are the result of the actions of a previous life. Blindness, poverty, hunger, physical deformity, outcastness and other social agonies are all the outworking of punishment for evil deeds in a previous existence.

It would follow that any attempt to alleviate such pain and misery would be an interference with the just ways of God. This concept is one reason why the Hindus did so little for so long for their unfortunates. Some enlightened Hindus today are talking about and working toward social progress and change, but they have not yet reconciled this new concept with the clear, ancient doctrine of Karma, which is basic to Hindu thought and life.

This Karma concept, however, does serve as a neat, simple, clearly understood explanation of suffering: suffering is all the result of previous evil-doing.

But is there not a sense in which it is true that Christianity also holds that suffering is punishment from God?

Certainly, in the minds of many, it is. "What did I do to deserve this?" is often the first question on the lips of a sufferer. And the conviction of friends, expressed or unexpressed, frequently operates on this same assumption. The classic treatment of the problem of suffering and evil in the book of Job shows how this cruel assumption was accepted by Job's friends. It compounded his already staggering pain.

It is clear from the teaching of both the Old and the New Testaments that suffering may be the judgment of God, but that there are many instances when it is totally unrelated to personal wrongdoing. An automatic assumption of guilt and consequent punishment is totally unwarranted.

To be sure, God is not a sentimental grandfather of the sky with a boys-will-be-boys attitude. "A man reaps what he sows" (Gal

6:7) is a solemn warning to any who would tweak God's nose in arrogant presumption. God afflicted Miriam with leprosy for challenging the authority of Moses, her brother whom God had appointed leader. He took the life of David's child, born of his adulterous relationship with Bathsheba.

Other examples could be cited. In the New Testament we have the startling example of Ananias and Sapphira, who were struck dead for lying, cheating and hypocrisy. That there may be a connection between suffering and sin is evident, but that it is not always so is abundantly clear. We have the unambiguous word of our Lord himself on the subject. The disciples apparently adhered to the direct retribution theory of suffering. One day when they saw a man who had been blind from birth they wanted to know who had sinned to cause this blindness—the man or his parents. Jesus made it clear that neither was responsible for his condition, "but this happened so that the work of God might be displayed in his life" (Jn 9:1-3).

On receiving word of some Galileans whom Pilate had slaughtered, Jesus went out of his way to point out that they were not greater sinners than other Galileans. He said that the eighteen people who had been killed when the tower of Siloam fell on them were not greater sinners than others in Jerusalem. From both incidents he made the point, "Unless you repent, you too will all perish" (Lk 13:1-3).

Clearly, then, we are jumping the gun if we assume automatically, either in our own case or in that of another that the explanation of any given tragedy or suffering is the judgment of God. Further, as Hopkins observes, it seems clear from biblical examples that if one's troubles are the just rewards of misdeeds, the sufferer is never left in any doubt when his trouble is a punishment.

Judgment Preceded by Warning
Indeed, one of the profound truths of the whole of Scripture is that

the judgment of God is preceded by warning. Throughout the Old Testament we have the repeated pleadings of God and warning of judgment. Only after warning is persistently ignored and rejected does judgment come. God's poignant words are an example. "I take no pleasure in the death of the wicked, but rather that they turn from their ways and live. Turn! Turn from your evil ways! Why will you die, O house of Israel?" (Ezek 33:11).

The same theme continues in the New Testament. What more moving picture of God's love and long-suffering is there than our Lord as he weeps over Jerusalem, "I have longed to gather your children together, as a hen gathers her chicks under her wings, but you were not willing" (Mt 23:37). And we have the clear word of Peter that the Lord does not want "anyone to perish, but everyone to come to repentance" (2 Pet 3:9).

When someone asks, "How could a good God send people to hell?" we should point out that, in a sense, God sends no one to hell. We send ourselves. God has done all that is necessary for us to be forgiven, redeemed, cleansed and made fit for heaven. All that remains is for us to receive this gift. If we refuse it, God has no option but to give us our choice. Heaven, for the person who does not want to be there, would be hell.

Though the judgment of God sometimes explains suffering there are several other possibilities to consider. People, as we saw earlier, were responsible for the coming of sin and death into the universe. We must not forget that humankind's wrongdoing is also responsible for a great deal of misery and suffering in the world today. Negligence in the construction of a building has sometimes resulted in its collapse in a storm, with consequent death and injury. How many lives have been snuffed out by the murder of drunken driving? The cheating, lying, stealing and selfishness which are so characteristic of our society today all reap a bitter harvest of suffering. But we can hardly blame God for it! Think of all the misery that has its origin in the wrongdoing of human beings—it is remarkable how much suffering is accounted for in this way.

The Presence of an Enemy

But we are not alone on this planet. By divine revelation we know of the presence of an enemy. He appears in various forms, we are told, appropriate to the occasion. He may appear as an angel of light or as a roaring lion, depending on the circumstances and his purposes. His name is Satan. It was he whom God allowed to cause Job to suffer. Jesus, in the Parable of the Good Seed and the Tares, explains the ruining of the farmer's harvest by saying, "An enemy did this" (Mt 13:28). Satan finds great pleasure in ruining God's creation and causing misery and suffering. God allows him limited power, but he cannot touch the one in close fellowship with God. "Resist the devil, and he will flee from you" (Jas 4:7), we are assured. Nevertheless, Satan accounts for some of the disease and suffering in the world today.

In answer to the question of why God allows Satan power to bring suffering, we can learn from Robinson Crusoe's answer to his man, Friday.

"Well," says Friday, "you say God is so strong, so great; has he not as much strong, as much might as the devil?"

"Yes, yes," says I; "Friday, God is much stronger than the devil."

"But if God much strong, much might as the devil why God no kill the devil so make him no more do wicked?'"

"You may as well ask," answers Crusoe reflectively, "why does God not kill you and me when we do wicked things that offend him?"

God Feels Our Suffering

In considering pain and suffering, whether it be physical or mental, another important consideration must be kept in mind. God is not a distant, aloof, impervious potentate, far removed from his people and their sufferings. He not only is aware of suffering—he *feels* it.

No pain or suffering has ever come to us that has not first passed through the heart and hand of God. However greatly we may suffer, it is well to remember that God is the great sufferer. Comforting are the words of Isaiah the prophet, foretelling the agony of Christ: "He was despised and rejected by men, a man of sorrows, and familiar with suffering" (Is 53:3). Another writer reminds us, "Because he himself suffered when he was tempted, he is able to help those who are being tempted" (Heb 2:18). And "We do not have a high priest who is unable to sympathize with our weaknesses, but we have one who has been tempted in every way, just as we are—yet was without sin" (Heb 4:15).

The problem of evil and suffering is one of the profound problems of the ages. It is becoming increasingly acute in our time, with the advent of the bomb. There are no easy answers, and we do not have the last word. There are, however, clues.

Risky Gift of Free Will

■ *First, evil is a necessary part of free will.* As J. B. Phillips has put it:

> Evil is inherent in the risky gift of free will. God could have made us machines but to do so would have robbed us of our precious freedom of choice, and we would have ceased to be human. Exercise of free choice in the direction of evil in what we call the "fall" of man, is the basic reason for evil and suffering in the world. It is man's responsibility, not God's. He could stop it, but in so doing would destroy us all. It is worth noting that the whole point of real Christianity lies not in interference with the human power to choose, but in producing a willing consent to choose good rather than evil.[3]

Unless the universe is without significance, the actions of every individual affects others. No one is an island. To have it otherwise would be like playing a game of chess and changing the rules after every move. Life would be meaningless.

■ *Second, much of the suffering in the world can be traced directly to the evil choices men and women make.* This is quite apparent when a bank robber kills someone. Sometimes it is less apparent and more indirect, as when crooked decisions are made in government or business that may bring deprivation and suffering to many people unknown to those who make the decisions. Even the results of natural disasters are sometimes compounded by people's culpability in refusing to heed warnings of their coming.

■ *Third, some—but not all—suffering is allowed by God as judgment and punishment.* This is a possibility which must always be considered. God usually allows such suffering with a view to restoration and character formation, and those suffering as a result of their deeds usually know it.

■ *Fourth, God has an implacable enemy in Satan.* He has been defeated at the cross but is free to work his evil deeds until the final judgment. That there is in the world a force of evil stronger than human beings is clear from revelation and from experience.

■ *Fifth, God himself is the great sufferer and has fully met the problem of evil in the gift of his own Son, at infinite cost to himself.* The consequence of evil for eternity is forever removed as we embrace the Lord Jesus Christ. Our sin is forgiven and we receive new life and power to *choose* what is right as the Holy Spirit forms the image of Christ in us.

Greatest Test of Faith

Perhaps the greatest test of faith for the Christian today is to believe that God is good. There is so much which, taken in isolation, suggests the contrary. Helmut Thielecke of Hamburg points out that a fabric viewed through a magnifying glass is clear in the middle and blurred at the edges. But we know the edges are clear because of what we see in the middle. Life, he says, is like a fabric. There are many edges which are blurred, many events and circumstances we do not understand. But they are to be interpreted by the clarity we see in the center—the cross of Christ. We are not left to guess about the goodness of God from isolated bits of data. He has clearly revealed his character and dramatically demonstrated it to us in the cross. "He who did not spare his own Son, but gave him up for us all—how will he not also, along with him, graciously give us all things?" (Rom 8:32).

God never asks us to understand; we need only trust him in the same way we ask that our child only trust our love, though he may not understand or appreciate a visit to the doctor.

Peace comes when we realize that we do not have the full picture.

Then we can affirm, with calm relief and joy, that in "all things God works for the good of those who love him" (Rom 8:28).

At times it is our reaction to suffering, rather than the suffering itself, that determines whether the experience is one of blessing or of blight. The same sun melts the butter and hardens the clay.

When by God's grace we can view all of life through the lens of faith in God's love, we can affirm with Habakkuk, "Though the fig tree does not bud and there are no grapes on the vines, though the olive crop fails and the fields produce no food, though there are no sheep in the pen and no cattle in the stalls, yet I will rejoice in the LORD, I will be joyful in God my Savior" (Hab 3:17-18).

For Individual or Group Study

1. In what instances do people lay blame unjustly on God for suffering and evil?

2. Can you think of any occasions when God was responsible for evil or suffering in Scripture, history or recent events? If so, what are some?

3. What would happen to the world we know if God completely stamped out evil (pp. 132-33)?

What prevents God from *occasionally* intervening in human affairs to combat evil or relieve suffering?

4. How has God already demonstrated that he wants to rid the world of suffering and evil (pp. 133-34)?

5. Do you see God doing this today? Would prayer cause him to do this more?

6. Would you prefer a world in which people were always rewarded for good and punished for evil (pp. 134-36)? Why or why not?

7. Scripture tells us that sometimes God rewards good and warns about and then punishes evil. How have you seen this in daily life?

8. Where is God when his creation suffers (pp. 138-39)?

9. The question of why God allows suffering and evil goes beyond *why* we believe in God to *what* we will believe about him. How does the answer to this question affect our Christian life?

10. "The same sun melts the butter and hardens the clay" (p. 141). Is there someone you know who seems to be like clay but is turning into butter? How can you represent Christ to that person?

11. In your own experience, has suffering brought you closer to God or alienated you from him?

12. If Christ were standing beside you, what would you tell him about your suffering or the injustice you see? What would you ask?

13. Take time now to add any new insights to your list of reasons for putting your hope in God through Christ Jesus.

For Further Reading

Lewis, C. S. *The Problem of Pain.* New York: Macmillan, 1978.

Murphree, Jon Tal. *A Loving God and a Suffering World.* Downers Grove, Ill.: InterVarsity Press, 1981.

Peterson, Michael. *Evil and the Christian God.* Grand Rapids, Mich.: Baker Book House, 1982.

Yancy, Philip. *Where Is God When It Hurts?* Grand Rapids, Mich.: Zondervan, 1977.

11
Does Christianity Differ from Other World Religions?
● ● ● ● ● ● ● ● ● ● ●

HOW CHRISTIANITY DIFFERS SIGNIFICANTLY FROM OTHER RE-
ligions is a subject often discussed in our shrinking modern world.
There is, currently, a meeting of cultures, nations, races and religions on a scale unprecedented in history. In this jet age we are
no more than twenty-four hours away from any spot on the earth.
Television brings into our living rooms the coronation of a pope,
the burning of a Buddhist monk and a Muslim ceremony conduc-
ted by a political leader.

Over 350,000 students from more than 180 countries of the
world come to the United States every year to study in more than
2,500 colleges and universities in every one of the 50 states.[1]
Brightly colored saris on graceful Indian women and striking tur-
bans on erect Sikhs are not unfamiliar sights in our metropolitan
areas or small college towns. In addition, there are multiplied

thousands of diplomatic, business and tourist visitors every year.

Many of these visitors find their way into parent-teacher organization meetings, service clubs and churches to speak on their cultural and religious backgrounds. They are sincere, educated and intelligent. They are often interested in learning about Christianity, and we may learn from them.

As one has contact with these friends from overseas and becomes aware of their religious beliefs, the question naturally arises as to whether or not Christianity is unique among world religions, or is it only a variation on a basic theme running through all religions? To put it another way, "Does not the sincere Muslim, Buddhist, Hindu or Jew worship the same God as we do, but under a different name?" Or, quite bluntly, "Is Jesus Christ the *only* way to God?"

In answering this question, it is extremely important that we first empty it of its potentially explosive emotional content. When a Christian asserts that Jesus Christ is the only way to God, and that apart from him there is no salvation, he or she is not suggesting that Christians think they are better than anyone else. Some people erroneously view Christians as having formed a bigots club, like a fraternity with a racial segregation clause. If only the fraternity and the Christians were less bigoted, such people think, they would vote to change their membership rules and, in the case of the Christians, let in anyone who believes in God. "Why bring Jesus Christ into it?" we are often asked. "Why can't we just agree on God?" And this brings us to the fundamental issue.

Christians assert that Jesus Christ is the only way to God because Scripture says, "Salvation is found in no one else, for there is no other name under heaven given to men by which we must be saved" (Acts 4:12). Christians believe this, not because they have made it *their* rule, but because Jesus Christ our Lord taught it (Jn 14:6). A Christian cannot be faithful to his Lord and affirm anything else. He is faced with the problem of truth. If Jesus Christ is who he claims to be, then we have the authoritative word of God himself on the subject. If he is God and there is no other Savior, then obviously he is the *only* way to God. Christians could not change this fact by a vote or by anything else.

It is helpful to point out, to those who ask this question, that there are some laws the penalty for which is socially determined. There are other laws of which this is not true. For instance, the penalty for driving through a stoplight is determined by society. It is not inherent in the act itself. The penalty could be set at fifty dollars or at ten dollars, or the law could be abolished completely.

With the law of gravity, however, the penalty for violation is not socially determined. People could vote to unanimously suspend the law of gravity for an hour, but no one in his right mind would jump off the roof to test it! No, the penalty for violating that law is inherent in the act itself, and the person who violated it would be picked up with a blotter despite the unanimous resolution!

As there are inherent physical laws, so there are inherent spiritual laws. One of them is God's revelation of himself in Christ. Another is Christ's death as the only atonement for sin.

In proclaiming the exclusiveness of Christ, a Christian does not assume a superior posture. He speaks as a sinner saved by grace. As D. T. Niles, of Ceylon, so beautifully put it, "Evangelism is just one beggar telling another beggar where to find food."

The Question of Truth

After defusing the emotional bomb, it is then important to move on to the important question of truth. Sincerely believing something does not make it true, as anyone will testify who has ever picked a wrong bottle out of a medicine cabinet in the dark. Faith is no more valid than the object in which it is placed, no matter how sincere or how intense the faith is. A nurse put carbolic acid in the eyes of a newborn baby, sincerely thinking she was applying silver nitrate. Her sincerity did not save the baby from blindness.

These same principles apply to things spiritual. Believing some thing doesn't make it true any more than failing to believe truth makes it false. Facts are facts, regardless of people's attitudes toward them. In religious matters, the basic question is always, "Is it true?"

Take, for instance, the fact of the deity, death and resurrection of the Lord Jesus Christ. Christianity affirms these facts as the heart of its message. Islam, on the other hand, denies the deity, death and resurrection of Christ. On this very crucial point, one of these mutually contradictory views is wrong. They can't simultaneously be true, no matter how sincerely both are believed by how many people.

A great deal is said about the similarity of world religions. Many Christians naively assume that other religions are basically the same, making the same claims and essentially doing what Christianity does, but in slightly different terms. Such an attitude reveals complete ignorance of the doctrines of other religions.

Though there are some similarities, the differences far outweigh, and are much greater than, the similarities.

Is the Golden Rule Enough?
One of the similarities is the essence of the Golden Rule, which is contained in almost every religion. From Confucius's time we have the statement in various forms, that we should do unto others as we would have others do unto us. Many wrongly assume that this is the essence of Christianity. But if all Jesus Christ did was to give us the Sermon on the Mount and the Golden Rule, he would have actually increased our frustration. As we have seen, we have had the Golden Rule since Confucius's time. Our problem has never been not knowing what we should do. Our problem, rather has been that we lack power to do what we know we should.

Christ raised the ethical level and thereby made the requirements higher. This by itself raises our frustration level. But that is not all Christ did, and this is a major difference between Christianity and other religions. Christ offers us his power to live as we should. He gives us forgiveness, cleansing and his own righteousness, all as a free gift. He reconciles us to God. He does something for us we cannot do for ourselves.

Every other religious system, however, is essentially a do-it-yourself proposition. Follow this way of life, they say, and you will gain favor with God and eventually achieve salvation. In a sense, other religious systems are sets of swimming instructions for a drowning man. Christianity is a life preserver.

A Free Gift

D. T. Niles has also observed that in other religions good works are an "in order to." In Christianity, they are a "therefore." In other religions, good works are the means by which one hopes to earn salvation. In Christianity salvation is received as a free gift, through the finished work of Christ, the "therefore" good works becomes an imperative love of God. Or, as another has put it, other religions are *do;* Christianity is *done.*

Christianity is what God has done for human beings in seeking them and reaching down to help them. Other religions are a matter of human beings seeking and struggling toward God.

Because of this profound difference, Christianity alone offers *assurance* of salvation. Because our salvation depends on what God has done for and given us, we can say with the same wonderful certainty as the apostle Paul, "To be away from the body . . . [is to be] at home with the Lord" (2 Cor 5:8).

No Assurance in a Works Religion

In every *works* religion, however, it is impossible ever to have assurance. When do you know that you have done enough good works? You *never* know, and never can know. Fear persists because there is no assurance of salvation.

What salvation is, and what we are pointing toward, is quite different in the world's religions from what it is in Christianity.

In Buddhism, for instance, the ultimate goal is nirvana, or the extinction of desire. According to Buddha's teaching, all pain and suffering come from desire. If this desire can be overcome by following the Eightfold Path to Enlightenment, one can achieve nirvana, which is total nothingness. It is likened to the snuffing out of a candle. This is said to happen to life and consciousness when nirvana has been achieved.

In Hinduism the ultimate goal is also nirvana, but the term here has a different meaning. Nirvana is ultimate reunion with Brahma, the all-pervading force of the universe which is the Hindu's God. This experience is likened to the return of a drop of water to the ocean. Individuality is lost in the reunion with God, but without the total self-annihilation of Buddhism. Nirvana, in Hinduism is achieved through a continuous cycle of birth, life, death and rebirth. As soon as any animal, insect, or human being dies, that being is immediatley reborn in another form. Whether one moves up or down the scale of life depends on the quality of moral life one has lived. If it has been a good life, one moves up the scale with more comfort and less suffering. If one has lived a bad life, one moves down the scale into suffering and poverty. If one has been bad enough, that person is not reborn as a human being at all but as an animal or insect. This law of reaping in the next life the harvest of one's present life is called the law of Karma. It explains why Hindus will not kill even an insect, not to mention a sacred cow, though these inhibitions pose grave sanitation and public health problems. What seems strange, curious and even ludicrous to us of the Western world has a very clear rationale to the Hindu.

In Islam heaven is thought of as a paradise of wine, women and song. It is achieved by living a life in which, ironically, one abstains from the things with which he or she will be rewarded in paradise. In addition to this abstention, one must follow the Five

Pillars of Islam: repeating the creed, making a pilgrimage to Mecca, giving alms to the poor, praying five times daily and keeping the fast of Ramadan.

Again, there is no possibility of assurance. I have often asked Hindus, Muslims and Buddhists whether they would achieve nirvana or go to paradise when they died. I have not yet had one reply in the affirmative. Rather, they referred to the imperfection of their lives as being a barrier to this realization. There is no assurance in their religious systems because there is no atonement, and salvation depends wholly on the individual's gaining enough merit.

Concept of God

Even the fundamental concept of God, on which there is a plea that we should agree, reveals wide divergences. To say that we can unite with all who believe in God, regardless of what this God is called, fails to recognize that the term *God* means nothing apart from the definition given it.

Buddha, contrary to popular belief, never claimed to be deity. In fact, he was agnostic about the whole question of whether God even existed. If God existed, the Buddha taught emphatically, he could not help an individual achieve enlightenment. Each person must work this out for himself or herself.

Hindus are pantheistic. *Pan* means all and *theistic* means God. Hindus believe that God and the universe are identical. The concept of *maya* is central to their thinking. Maya means that the material world is an illusion and that reality is spiritual and invisible. Brahma is the impersonal, all-pervading force of the universe, and the ultimate goal is for people to be reunited with this God in nirvana. Buddhism also teaches that the material world is an illusion. It is readily apparent why science came to birth through Christians, who believed in a personal God and an orderly universe, rather than in the context of Oriental philosophy. It is clear why most scientific progress has come from the West rather than the

East. Why would one investigate what he believes is an illusion?

In Islam and Judaism we have a God much closer to the Christian concept. Here God is personal and transcendent, or separate from his creation. Surely, we are urged, we may get together with those who believe in God in personal terms.

But as we examine the Muslim concept of God—Allah as he is called in the Koran—we find he is not the God and Father of Jesus Christ, but rather, as in all other instances, a God of people's own imagination. Our knowledge of Allah comes from the Koran, which came through Muhammad. Muhammad, like Buddha and unlike Jesus Christ, did not claim deity. He taught that he was only the prophet of Allah. The picture of God which comes through to us in the pages of the Koran is of one who is totally removed from men, one who is capricious in all of his acts, responsible for evil as well as for good, and who is certainly not the God who "so loved the world that he gave his one and only Son, that whoever believes in him shall not perish but have eternal life" (Jn 3:16). It is this totally distant concept of God that makes the idea of the Incarnation utterly inconceivable to the Muslim. How could their god, so majestic and beyond, have contact with mortal human beings in sin and misery? The death of God the Son on the cross is likewise inconceivable to a Muslim, since this would mean God was defeated by his creatures, an impossibility to them.

The Jewish God Is Close

The Jewish concept of God is closest of all to the Christian. Isn't the God whom they worship the God of the Old Testament, which we accept? Surely we can get together on this!

Again, however, closer examination shows that the Jews would not admit their God was the Father of Jesus Christ. In fact, it was this very issue that precipitated such bitter controversy in our Lord's time. God we accept, they said to Jesus Christ, but we do not accept you because as a man you are claiming yourself to be

God, which is a clear case of blasphemy.

In a conversation with the Jews, our Lord discussed this question. "God is our Father," they said. Jesus said to them, "If God were your Father, you would love me, for I came from God. . . . He who belongs to God hears what God says. The reason you do not hear is that you do not belong to God" (Jn 8:42, 47). In even stronger words he says, "You belong to your father, the devil" (v. 44).

Here, in our Lord's own words, we have the clue as to what our attitude should be toward those who are sincerely seeking *God.* If they are seeking the true God, their sincerity will be evidenced by the fact that they will receive Christ when they hear about him. Missionary history has numerous examples of those who have been following other gods and an unknown god but who have responded when presented with the truth about the Lord Jesus Christ. They have immediately realized that he is the true God, whom they have been seeking.

Scripture is clear throughout both the Old Testament and the New Testament that worship of gods other than the true God originates with the devil. "They must no longer offer any of their sacrifices to the goat idols" (Lev 17:7), and "The sacrifices of pagans are offered to demons, not to God" (1 Cor 10:20).

Christ Alone Claims Deity

Of the great religious leaders of the world, Christ alone claims deity. It really doesn't matter what one thinks of Muhammad, Buddha or Confucius as individuals. Their followers emphasize their teachings. Not so with Christ. He made *himself* the focal point of his teaching. The central question he put to his listeners was, "Whom do you say that *I* am?" When asked what doing the works of God involved, Jesus replied, "The work of God is this: to believe in the one he has sent" (Jn 6:29).

On the question of who and what God is, the nature of salvation and how it is obtained, it is clear that Christianity differs radically from other world religions. We live in an age in which tolerance is a key word. Tolerance, however, must be clearly understood. (Truth, by its very nature, is intolerant of error.) If two plus two is four, the total at the same time cannot be twenty-three. But one is not regarded as intolerant because he disagrees with *this* answer and maintains that the only correct answer is *four.*

The same principle applies in religious matters. One must be tolerant of other points of view and respect their right to be held and heard. He cannot, however, be forced in the name of tolerance to agree that all points of view, including those that are mutually contradictory, are equally valid. Such a position is nonsense.

The Only Way to God
It is not true that "it doesn't matter what you believe as long as you believe it." Hitler's slaughter of six million Jews was based on a sincere view of race supremacy, but he was desperately wrong. What we believe must be true in order to be real. Jesus said, "I am the way and the truth and the life. No one comes to the Father except through me" (Jn 14:6). There are many ways to Christ, but if we are to know the true and living God in personal experience, it must be through Christ, the only way to God.

For Individual or Group Study
1. Many people believe that all religions worship the same God but call that God by different names. To refute this claim, Paul Little briefly outlines four world religions—Buddhism, Hinduism, Islam and Christianity (pp. 148-50). Take time to summarize the chief points of each religion, including the religion's ultimate goal, method of achieving that goal and concept of a deity.

2. What are the greatest similarities between Christianity and these other religions? the greatest differences (pp. 151-52)?

3. Paul Little cautions against two faulty thoughts and attitudes: (1) snobbishness that makes it sound as if we *choose* to make Christianity the only way to God; and (2) an intellectual tolerance that believes that "all points of view, including those that are mutually contradictory, are equally valid" (p. 152). In

a discussion of world religions with a non-Christian, how could you keep from falling into either trap?

4. Taking these points into account, what is the value of comparing religions to see which is better (provides assurance of salvation, has done most for society, offers a palatable explanation for evil in the world, and so on)?

5. Should such comparisons affect how a person chooses a religion? defends a religion? Explain.

6. The author states: "In a conversation with the Jews, our Lord discussed [whether God was Jesus' Father]. 'God is our Father,' they said. Jesus said to them, . . . 'You are of your father, the devil' (Jn 8:44). Here, in our Lord's own words, we have the clue as to what our attitude should be toward those who are sincerely seeking *God*. If they are seeking the true God, their sincerity will be evidenced by the fact that they will receive Christ when they hear about him" (p. 151). Is sincerity the only prerequisite for being able to accept Christ? Explain.

7. What types of healing may need to take place before you or some sincere seekers will find Christ or trust him fully?

8. Take time now to add any new insights to your list of reasons for putting your hope in God through Christ Jesus. Space is provided following page 173.

For Further Reading

Anderson, Norman. *Christianity and World Religions,* 2nd ed. Downers Grove, Ill.: InterVarsity Press, 1984.

Enroth, Ronald M. *A Guide to Cults and New Religions.* Downers Grove, Ill.: InterVarsity Press, 1984.

Neill, Stephen. *Christian Faith and Other Faiths.* Downers Grove, Ill.: InterVarsity Press, 1984.

Newbigin, Lesslie. *The Finality of Christ.* Richmond, Va.: John Knox, 1969.

Sire, James W. *The Universe Next Door, Revised Edition.* Downers Grove, Ill.: InterVarsity Press, 1988.

12
Is Christian Experience Valid?
●●●●●●●●●●●

YOU COULD GET THE SAME RESPONSE FROM THAT TABLE LAMP IF you believed it possessed the same attributes as your God," said the young law student. This articulate skeptic was telling me what thousands feel—that Christian experience is completely personal and subjective and has no objective, eternal and universal validity.

The premise behind this notion is that the mind is capable of infinite rationalization. Belief in God is seen as mere wish fulfillment. In adults, it is a throwback to our need for a father image.

The assumption, whether expressed or not, is that Christianity is for emotional cripples who can't make it through life without a crutch.

It is claimed that Christian conversion is a psychologically in-auced experience brought about by *brainwashing* as used by both Fascists and Communists. An evangelist is just a master of psychological manipulation. After pounding away at an audience, he finds that people become putty in his hands. He can get them to do anything if he asks for a *decision* at the right time and in the right way.

Some go further. Christian experience, they claim, is sometimes positively harmful. More than one student has been packed off to a psychiatrist by unbelieving parents after he or she has come to personal faith in Christ. "Look at all the religious nuts in mental asylums. It's their religion that put them there." Those who feel this way have succumbed to the "common-factor fallacy" pointed out by Anthony Standen. He tells of a man who got drunk each Monday on whiskey and soda water; on Tuesday he got drunk on brandy and soda water; and Wednesday on gin and soda water. What caused the drunkenness? Obviously the common factor, soda water![1]

The Last Stop on the Train

For many, the church is thought of as the last stop on the train before being institutionalized. A careful scrutiny of a truly disoriented person, however, would reveal imbalance and unreality in other areas as well as in his religious life. It is actually a credit to the church that she offers help to these people. On the other hand, some mental disturbances have spiritual roots. As these people come into a right relationship with God, through Jesus Christ they find release and healing.

So strong is the prejudice in some quarters against the validity of Christian experience that academic degrees have been denied. A friend, studying in one of our best-known universities, was denied a Ph.D. degree in social science. He was told, "Believing what you do about God, you are by definition crazy."

It is suggested by some skeptics that all Christian experience can be explained on the basis of conditioned reflexes. This thinking has its roots in experiments by Pavlov, the famous Russian scientist. He placed measuring devices in a dog's mouth and stomach to determine the production of digestive juices. Then he would bring food to the dog and at the same time ring a bell. After doing this repeatedly over a period of time, Pavlov rang the bell without producing the food and the dog salivated as usual. The inference drawn is that by such repeated conditioning, the mind can be made to produce desired physical reactions. It is on this basis that we can explain all political, social and religious conversions, say the proponents of this view.

These are serious, far-reaching charges. Some of them have an air of plausibility.

Is Christian Experience Valid?

At the outset, we must concede the possibility of manipulating human emotions in some circumstances. And we would have to admit that some evangelists consciously or unconsciously play on the emotions of their audiences with deathbed stories, histrionic performances and other devices. Our Lord, in the Parable of the Sower, implicitly warns against merely stirring the emotions in evangelism. He describes those who have received the seed of the Word into stony places as those that have heard the Word and received it with joy but who have no roots in themselves. They endure until tribulation and persecution come, and then they are *soon offended.* All of us have known people who have made what appears to be a tremendous response to the gospel, only to find later that they have fallen by the wayside. Often this happens when they learn that it costs something to be a Christian and are not prepared to pay the price. Their emotions are stirred but their wills have not been bent to obey the Lord in total commitment.

A Matter of the Will

Dr. Orville S. Walters, a Christian psychiatrist, has pointed out that the will is like a cart pulled by two horses, the emotions and the intellect. With some people the will is reached more quickly through the emotions. With others it is reached through the mind. But in every case there is no genuine conversion unless the will has been involved.[2]

Realizing these potentialities for manipulating emotions, even unconsciously, all who are involved in evangelistic work, whether with children or with adults, must eliminate, so far as is humanly possible, factors and techniques which could produce these abortive results. But to attempt to explain all Christian experience on a psychological basis does not fit the facts. In passing, it is well to observe a principle that applies here as well as in other areas: to describe something is not the same thing as explaining it. To be sure, Christian experience can be described psychologically, but this does not explain *why* it happens nor negate its reality.

One evidence that Christianity is true is the reality of the experience of those who embrace Jesus Christ. One of the challenges a Christian throws out to skeptics is, "Taste and see that the LORD is good" (Ps 34:8). Verify for yourself, in the laboratory of life, the hypothesis that Jesus Christ is the living Son of God. The reality of Christian experience is evidence of the validity of Christianity.

A Conditioned Reflex?

What of the objections that Christian experience is merely a conditioned reflex? First we must ask, as Dr. D. Martyn Lloyd-Jones does in answering the influential book *Battle for the Mind,* by William Sargant, whether the comparison between people and animals is a strictly legitimate one. A human being has reason and a critical faculty, and has powers of self-analysis, self-contemplation and self-criticism which make him or her quite different from animals. "In other words, the comparison is only valid at times (like war) when what differentiates man has been knocked out of action and a man, because of terrible stress, has been reduced for the time being to the level of an animal."[3]

Second, if we are only creatures of conditioned reflexes, then this must also explain acts of great heroism and self-sacrifice in which human beings have taken pride. Such acts must be nothing but responses to a given stimulus at a given point. Taken to its logical conclusion, a deterministic view of human behavior eliminates moral responsibility. The little girl who said, "It ain't my fault; it's my glands," would be right. It is significant, however, that those holding a deterministic point of view philosophically tend to operate on a different basis in daily life: like anyone else, they want a pickpocket arrested promptly!

We cannot explain Christian experience on a conditioned reflex basis, however. Since thousands reared in Christian homes unfortunately never become Christians, the fact that many others really trust Christ cannot be explained exclusively on the basis of background. Though personal faith in Christ is the only door to becoming a Christian, the roads that lead to that door are almost as many as the number who enter it. I have known persons who became Christians the first time they heard the gospel. It is significant, by contrast, that in political brainwashing, as with Pavlov's experiments, the stimulus must be applied repeatedly for some time in order to get the desired result.

Those who have become Christians, out of every conceivable religious background and out of no background at all, testify uniformly to an experience through personal commitment to Jesus Christ. The evidence of their changed lives testifies to the reality of the experience. This result cannot be gained from a bridge lamp by positive thinking. If positive thinking were the answer to everything, we would have no problems. As a matter of fact, the law student previously referred to committed his life to Christ in the course of the week's lectures that followed.

Victims of Autohypnosis?

But how do we Christians know that we are not victims of autohypnosis? How do we know we are not just whistling in the dark? Subjective experience as such does not prove anything. Many have claimed experience—the reality of which we may legitimately question. There must be more than experience on which to base our conviction, or we could be in difficulty.

For instance, suppose a man with a fried egg over his left ear came through the door of your church. "Oh," he says, glowing, "this egg really gives me joy, peace, purpose in life, forgiveness of sins and strength for living!" What would you say to him? You can't tell him he hasn't experienced these things. One of the powers of personal testimony is that it can't be argued. The blind man mentioned in John 9 couldn't answer many of the questions put to him, but he was sure of the fact that now he could see. His testimony was eloquent in its power.

But we could ask several questions of our friend with the fried egg. These are questions we Christians must also be prepared to answer.

First, who else has had the same experience with the fried egg? Presumably our friend would be hard put to produce others. The late Harry Ironside was preaching some years ago when a heckler shouted, "Atheism has done more for the world than Christianity!"

"Very well," said Ironside, "tomorrow night you bring a hundred men whose lives have been changed for the better by atheism, and I'll bring a hundred who have been transformed by Christ."

Needless to say, his heckler friend did not appear the next night. With Christianity, there are hundreds from every race, every country and every walk of life who bear testimony to an experience through Jesus Christ.

Second, we should ask our friend with the fried egg: What objective reality outside of himself is his internal subjective experience tied to? How does he know he is not a victim of autohypnosis? Of course he will have nothing to say. In Christianity our personal subjective experience is tied into the objective historical fact of the resurrection of Christ. If Christ had not risen from the dead we would not experience him. It's because he rose from the dead and is living today that we can actually know him.

Objective Historical Fact

Christian experience is not induced by belief in unrealities. It is not like the fraternity boy who died of fright when tied to a railroad track one night during hazing. He was told that a train would be coming in five minutes. He was not told that the train would pass on a parallel track. He thought there was only one track. When he heard the train approaching he suffered heart failure. With Christianity, nothing happens if there is "no one out there."

Because Christ is really there, all the possibilities of his life within us are realizable. It is only half the story when we sing, "He lives within my heart." The other crucial half is that we know he lives because he rose from the dead in history. Our personal subjective experience is based on objective historical fact.

In commenting on the truth that people, in suffering, speak of drawing upon power outside themselves, J. B. Phillips says:

I know perfectly well that I am merely describing subjective phenomena. But the whole point is that what I have observed results in *objective* phenomena—courage, faith, hope, joy and patience, for instance—and these qualities are very readily observed. The man who wants everything proved by scientific means is quite right in his insistence on "laboratory conditions" if he is investigating, shall we say, water-divining, clairvoyance or telekinesis. But there can be no such thing as "laboratory conditions" for investigating the realm of the human spirit unless it can be seen that the "laboratory conditions" are in fact human life itself. A man can only exhibit objectively a change in his own disposition, a faith which directs his life—*in the actual business of living.*[4]

It is in these objective results in personal life that we see some of the dynamic relevance of Christ. He meets us in our deepest needs.

Purpose and Direction
Christ gives purpose and direction to life. "I am the light of the world," he says. "Whoever follows me will never walk in darkness but will have the light of life" (Jn 8:12). Many are in the dark about the purpose of life in general and about their own lives in particular. They are groping around the room of life looking for the light switch. Anyone who has ever been in a dark, unfamiliar room knows this feeling of insecurity. When the light goes on, however, a feeling of security results. And so it is when one steps from darkness to the light of life in Christ.

God in Christ gives our lives cosmic purpose, tying them in with his purpose for history and eternity. A Christian lives not only for time, but for eternity. Even routine is transformed as we live the whole of our lives in God's purpose and obey the admonition, "Whether you eat or drink or whatever you do, do it all for the glory of God" (1 Cor 10:31). This purpose embraces every aspect of life. It is also an unending, eternal purpose. Undoubtedly a non-Christian has such temporary purposes as family, career and money that give limited satisfaction. But these, at best, are transient and may fail with a change in circumstances.

To an age in which life has been described as meaningless and absurd by existentialist philosophers, nothing could have more power and meaning than this verifiable claim of Christ.

We Have Been Made for God
The late Carl Gustav Jung said, "The central neurosis of our time is emptiness." When we do not have money, fame, success, power, and other externals, we think we'll achieve final happiness after we attain them. Many testify to the disillusionment experienced when these have been achieved and the realization sets in that one is still the same miserable person. The human spirit can never be satisfied

"by bread alone"—by material things. We have been made for God and can find rest only in him.

An automobile, however shiny, high-powered and full of equipment, will not run on water. It was made to run only on gasoline. So people can find fulfillment only in God. We were made this way by God himself. Christian experience offers this fulfillment in a personal relationship to Christ. He said, "I am the bread of life. He who comes to me will never go hungry, and he who believes in me will never be thirsty" (Jn 6:35). When one experiences Christ, he or she comes to an inner contentment, joy and spiritual refreshment which enables him or her to transcend circumstances. It was this reality that enabled Paul to say, "I have learned to be content whatever the circumstances" (Phil 4:11). This supernatural reality enables a Christian to rejoice in the middle of difficult circumstances.

Our Quest Is for Peace

"Peace in our time" expresses the longing of each of us as we view the international scene. We hope against hope that the current brush-fire wars will not erupt into a large-scale conflict.

Peace is the quest of every human heart. If it could be bought, people would pay millions for it. The skyrocketing sales of books dealing with peace of mind and soul testify that they have touched a resonant chord in the lives of millions. Psychiatrists' offices are jammed.

Jesus says, "Come to me, all you who are weary and burdened, and I will give you rest" (Mt 11:28). Christ alone gives peace that passes understanding, a peace the world cannot give or take away. It is very moving to hear the testimony of those who have restlessly searched for years and have finally found peace in Christ. The current rise in narcotic addiction, alcoholism and sex obsession are vain hopes of gaining the peace which is in Christ alone. "He himself is our peace" (Eph 2:14).

A Radical Power Needed

Today's society is experiencing a profound power failure—a moral power failure. Parents know what is right for themselves and their children, but for lack of backbone they find it easier to go along with the crowd. Children readily pick up this attitude. The result is rapid deterioration of the moral fabric of society. Merely to give good advice to either the old or young is like putting iodine on cancer. What is needed is radical power. Christianity is not the putting of a new suit on a man, but the putting of a new man into the suit. Jesus Christ said, "I have come that they may have life, and have it to the full" (Jn 10:10). He offers us his power. Not only is there power and freedom from things like alcohol and narcotics, but power to forgive those who have wronged us, to resist temptation and to love the unlovely. Twice-born people have new appetites, new desires, new loves. They are, in fact, "new creations" (2 Cor 5:17). Salvation in reality is a literal coming from death to spiritual life.

Guilt Problem Solved

Christian experience solves the guilt problem. Every normal person feels guilt. A guilt complex is an irrational feeling that has no basis in fact. But guilt felt over something done wrongly, in violation of an inherent moral law, is normal. The absence of any guilt feeling is abnormal. A person who feels nothing after deliberately killing or hurting an innocent person is abnormal. Guilt must not be rationalized away. In Christ, there is an objective basis for forgiveness. Christ died for our sins; the sentence of death that belonged to us has been taken by him. "Therefore, there is now no condemnation for those who are in Christ Jesus" (Rom 8:1). Forgiveness at the personal level is a reality.

Christianity speaks to man's loneliness, which is so characteristic of modern society. It is ironic that in a period of population explosion man is more lonely than ever. Christ is the Good Shepherd (Jn 10:14) who will never leave us nor forsake us. And he introduces us into a worldwide family and a fellowship closer than a blood-relationship with an unbeliever.[5]

Conversion Affects Personality

Finally, in recognizing the validity of Christian experience we should realize that a psychological description of it is valid as far as it goes. But it is only a *description,* not a *cause.* A person who is converted has a new spiritual life within. This new life will thoroughly affect the person's entire personality. One part of a person's nature cannot be altered without affecting the rest of the person.

One's brain and nervous system may be analyzed in the same way as one's heart and kidney. The body and spirit are inextricably intertwined. The person is this totality. One is not merely a spirit encased in a body. On the other hand, one's mind is a reality.

The mechanical and spiritual aspects of life are complementary. Dr. Donald M. MacKay puts it very helpfully:

One familiar illustration is that of the use of lamps to signal from ships at sea. When a man sends a message from ship to shore, in one sense all that is coming from the ship is a series of flashes of light, but the trained sailor who sits on the shore watching this light says, "I see a message ordering so-and-so to proceed somewhere," or "Look, they're in trouble!" Why does he say this? All he has seen is "nothing but" flashes of light. The whole pattern of activity can be correctly labeled thus by a physicist, and described so completely that he is able to reproduce at any time exactly what the man on shore saw. He does not add "the message" as a kind of "extra" at the end of his description, and it would clearly be silly to say he is "leaving out the message" as if it were very wrong of him to do so. What he has done is to choose one way of approaching a complex unity, namely the sending-of-a-message-from-ship-to-shore, one aspect of which is a purely physical description in such terms as the wavelengths of the light and the time pattern. On the other hand, if he reads it also as a message, it is not as if he had found something mysterious, as well as the flashing, going on. Instead he has discovered that the whole thing, when he allows it to strike him in a different way, can be read and can also make sense in nonphysical terms. The message here is related to the flashing of light, not as an effect is to a cause, but rather as one aspect of a complex unity is related to another aspect.

Take another illustration. Two mathematicians start arguing about a problem in geometry. With a piece of chalk, they make a pattern of dots and lines on the board, and the fun waxes fast and furious. Can we imagine some nonmathematician coming in and saying, in amazement, "I can't see what you're arguing about—there's nothing there but chalk"? Once again this would illustrate what I like to call the fallacy of "nothing-buttery"— the idea that because, in one sense, at one level, or viewed from one angle, there is nothing there but chalk therefore it is un- necessary . . . to talk about what is there in any other terms. Again, if the mathematicians protest, "But there is a geometrical figure there; we are talking about these angles," they are not suggesting that the other man's eyes are failing to detect some- thing that they are seeing on the board. Both of them are re- sponding to exactly the same light waves. It is not that the mathematicians have a sixth sense or anything queer that ena- bles them to receive from the board some invisible emanations that the other fellow is not receiving. The point is that, as a result of a different attitude to what is there, they have power to see in it, or, if you like to abstract from it, an aspect of significance which the other misses. Of course, in this case he can be trained to discover it. There is no great difficulty in their eventually coming to agreement, and he then realizes that the geometrical pattern is related to the chalk on the board, not indeed as effect is to a cause, but in a still more intimate way.

I want to clarify this alternative to "a cause and effect," because it bears on questions that are often raised about the "causation" of bodily action by mental activity. If an argument were to come up as to whether the light causes the message or the message causes the light, whether the chalk-distribution causes the geometrical figure or the geometrical figure causes the chalk-distribution, we would see at once that the word "cause," in the scientific sense, is the wrong one here. Causality in science is a relationship between two events or sets of events, the cause and the effect. Here we have not two events or situations, but one. You cannot have the flashing of the light without the message: they are one set of events. You cannot have the chalk- distribution without there being, at the same time, the figure on the board. On the other hand, the two do have a certain kind of independence. It would be possible to reproduce the same message or figure in a quite different embodiment— in ink or pencil, for example. It is for this reason that I prefer to say that the one "embodies" the other.[6]

As Christians, we need not fear psychological descriptions of Christian experience. They are not explanations. The fact that some Christian experiences can be produced by other means is a warning against the temptation to manipulate human personality. The fact that solid Christian experience is also sound mental health is an asset rather than a detriment and is an evidence of the gospel's validity.

For Individual or Group Study

1. What are common ways non-Christians rationalize away the Christian experience (pp. 155-59)?

2. What is the "common-factor fallacy" (p. 156)?

3. In recent years, how have society and the media used it to discredit the Christian experience?

4. Christians often use these same presuppositions to understand people of

other religions. Why is this so?

5. Could one hundred atheists be found whose lives have been changed for the better by atheism (p. 160)? Is this a valid argument for or against atheism? Why?

6. What gives the Christian experience greater validity than the person in Paul Little's example who believes the fried egg on his ear had brought him joy, peace, purpose in life, forgiveness of sins and strength for living (p. 160)?

7. What would you say to the person who sincerely accepts Christ as Savior and Lord but doesn't feel the joy, peace, purpose in life, forgiveness of sins and strength for living that should accompany a Christian conversion experience?

8. Do you know someone who was drawn to Christ not because of the intellectual evidence for Christ but because Christianity seemed to benefit the lives of others? What Scripture passages would negate or validate this way to meet Christ?

9. How could you effectively present some of the truths in this chapter to a person who thinks your Christian experience is a fantasy?

10. Take time now to add any new insights to your list of reasons for putting your hope in God through Christ Jesus. Space is provided following page 173.

For Further Reading

Farmer, Herbert H. "The Psychological Theory of Religion." In *Towards Belief in God.* New York: Macmillan, 1978.

Rowe, William L. "Freud and Religious Belief." In *Philosophy of Religion: An Introduction.* Belmont, Calif.: Wadsworth, 1978.

Notes

Chapter 1: Is Christianity Rational?

[1]John W. Montgomery, "The Place of Reason," *HIS*, March 1966, p. 16.

[2]Antony Flew, "Theology and Falsification," *New Essays in Philosophical Theology*, eds. Antony Flew and Alasdair MacIntyre (London: SCM Press, 1955), n.p.

[3]On the issue of theological verification, see John W. Montgomery, "Inspiration and Inerrancy: A New Departure," *Evangelical Theological Society Bulletin* 8 (Spring 1956): 45-75.

Chapter 2: Is There a God?

[1]Mortimer Adler, *Great Books of the Western World,* ed. Robert Maynard Hutchins, vol. 2 (Chicago: Encyclopaedia Britannica, 1952), p. 561.

[2]Samuel Zwemer, *The Origin of Religion* (Neptune, N.J.: Loizeaux Bros., 1945).

[3]R. C. Sproul, *Reason to Believe* (Grand Rapids, Mich.: Lamplighter Books, 1978), p. 112.

[4]Lincoln Barnett, *The Universe and Dr. Einstein* (New York: Bantam, 1974), p. 95.

[5]Sir Fred Hoyle, *The Intelligent Universe* (London: Michael Joseph, 1983), pp. 11-12, 19, 251.

[6]Robert Gange, *Origins and Destiny* (Waco, Tex.: Word Books, 1986), p. 39.

[7]Bernard Ramm, *The Christian View of Science and Scripture* (Grand Rapids, Mich.: Eerdmans, 1954), p. 148.

[8]R. E. D. Clark, *Creation* (London: Tyndale Press, 1946), p. 20.

[9]Richard Lewontin, "Adaptation," *Scientific American,* vol. 239, no. 3, p. 212.

[10]James Brooks, *Origins of Life* (Belleville, Mich.: Lion/Tring, 1985), pp. 109-10.

[11]Robert Jastrow, *God and the Astronomers* (New York; London: W. W. Norton, 1978), pp. 12-14, 116.

[12]William Lane Craig, *The Existence of God and the Beginning of the Universe* (San Bernardino, Calif.: Here's Life Pub., 1979), pp. 59-60.

[13]Jastrow, *God and the Astronomers,* pp. 11, 14, 113-14.

[14]C. S. Lewis, *Mere Christianity* (New York: Macmillan, 1943), pp. 3, 11, 15-19.

Chapter 3: Is Christ God?

[1]John R. W. Stott, *Basic Christianity* (Downers Grove, Ill.: InterVarsity Press, 1964), p. 26.

[2]C. S. Lewis, "Miracles," in Stott, *Basic Christianity,* p. 32.

[3]Bernard Ramm, *Protestant Christian Evidences* (Chicago: Moody Press, 1953), p. 177.

Chapter 4: Did Christ Rise from the Dead?

[1]David Strauss, *The Life of Jesus for the People,* 2nd ed. (London, 1879), 1:412.

[2]B. F. Westcott, *The Gospel of the Resurrection,* 4th ed. (London, 1879), pp. 4-6.

Chapter 5: Is the Bible God's Word?

[1]B. B. Warfield, *The Inspiration and Authority of the Bible* (New York: Oxford University Press, 1927), pp. 299ff.

[2]Gordon Clark, *Can I Trust My Bible?* (Chicago: Moody Press, 1963), pp. 15-16.

[3]E. J. Carnell, *An Introduction to Christian Apologetics* (Grand Rapids, Mich.: Eerdmans, 1950), p. 208.

[4]Clark, *Can I Trust My Bible?* p. 27.

Chapter 6: Are the Bible Documents Reliable?

[1]R. Laird Harris, "How Reliable Is the Old Testament Text?" in Gordon Clark, *Can I Trust My Bible?* (Chicago: Moody Press, 1963), p. 124.

[2]Ibid., pp. 129-30.

[3]B. F. Westcott and F. J. A. Hort, eds., vol. 2, *New Testament in Original Greek* (London, 1881), p. 2.

[4]F. F. Bruce, *The New Testament Documents; Are They Reliable?* (Grand Rapids, Mich.: Eerdmans, 1959). Contains a full discussion of the dating of documents.

[5]Ibid., pp. 16-17.

[6]Ibid., p. 19.

[7]A. Berkley Mickelsen, "Is the Text of the New Testament Reliable?" in Clark,

Can I Trust My Bible? p. 160.

[8]Sir Frederic Kenyon, "The Bible and Archaeology," in Bruce, *New Testament Documents,* p. 20.

[9]E. J. Young, "The Canon of the Old Testament," in *Revelation and the Bible,* ed. C. F. Henry (Grand Rapids, Mich.: Baker Book House, 1956), p. 156.

Chapter 7: Does Archaeology Verify the Truth of Scripture?

[1]W. F. Albright, "Archaeology and the Religion of Israel," in Howard F. Vos, *An Introduction to Bible Archaeology* (Chicago: Moody Press, n.d.), p. 121.

[2]Millar Burrows, "What Mean These Stones?" in Vos, *Bible Archaeology.*

[3]Ibid., pp. 291-92.

[4]H. Darrell Lance, *The Old Testament and the Archaeologist* (Philadelphia, Pa.: Fortress Press, 1981), p. 65.

[5]A. R. Millard, *The Bible B.C.* (Phillipsburg, N.J.: Presbyterian and Reformed Publishing Co., 1982), p. 9.

[6]A. Rendle Short, *Modern Discovery and the Bible* (London: Inter-Varsity Christian Fellowship, 1949), p. 137.

[7]Millard, *The Bible B.C.,* pp. 9-10.

[8]A. R. Millard, *Treasures from Bible Times* (Tring; Belleville; Sydney: A Lion Book, 1985), pp. 54-57.

[9]Edwin M. Yamauchi, *The Stones and the Scripture* (Philadelphia; New York: Lippencott, 1972), p. 38.

[10]Ibid., p. 39.

[11]Millard, *Treasures,* pp. 47-48.

[12]Yamauchi, *Stones,* p. 68.

[13]Millard, *The Bible,* p. 25

[14]Ibid, p. 27.

[15]Short, *Modern Discovery,* p. 184.

[16]Millard, *The Bible,* p. 29.

[17]F. F. Bruce, "Archaeological Confirmation of the New Testament," in *Revelation and the Bible,* ed. C. F. Henry (Grand Rapids, Mich.: Baker Book House, 1958), p. 320.

[18]Ibid., p. 323.

[19]Ibid., p. 324.

[20]Ibid., p. 327.

[21]Keith N. Schoville, *Biblical Archaeology in Focus* (Grand Rapids, Mich.: Baker Book House, 1978), p. 156.

Chapter 8: Are Miracles Possible?

[1]J. N. Hawthorne, *Questions of Science and Faith* (London: Tyndale Press, 1960), p. 55.

[2]Bernard Ramm, *Protestant Evidences* (Chicago: Moody Press, 1953), p. 140.

[3]Ibid., pp. 140-41.

[4]Ibid., p. 142-43.

[5]C. S. Lewis, "Miracles," in Ramm, *Christian Evidences*, p. 143.

[6]Ramm, *Christian Evidences*, p. 160.

[7]Ibid., p. 40.

Chapter 9: Do Science and Scripture Agree?

[1]*U.S. News & World Report*, Inc. (Dec. 1, 1980): 62.

[2]Quoted in *Christianity Today* (Oct. 8, 1982): 38.

[3]J. N. Hawthorne, *Questions of Science and Faith* (London: Tyndale Press, 1960), p. 4.

[4]G. A. Kerkut, *The Implications of Evolution* (London: Pergamon Press, 1960), p. 20.

[5]Kenneth S. Kantzer, "Guideposts for the Current Debate Over Origins," *Christianity Today* (Oct. 8, 1982): 23, 26.

[6]A. E. Wilder-Smith, *The Natural Sciences Know Nothing of Evolution* (San Diego, Calif.: Master Books, 1981), p. 131.

[7]Francis A. Schaeffer, *No Final Conflict* (Downers Grove, Ill.: InterVarsity Press, 1975), p. 16.

[8]Davis A. Young, "An Ancient Earth Is Not a Problem; Evolutionary Man Is," *Christianity Today* (Oct. 8, 1982): 42.

[9]Kantzer, "Guideposts," p. 26.

[10]W. A. Criswell, *The Bible for Today's World* (Grand Rapids, Mich.: Zondervan, 1966), p. 30.

[11]Kerkut, *Implications*, p. 3.

Chapter 10: Why Does God Allow Suffering and Evil?

[1]Hugh Evan Hopkins, "Mystery of Suffering," (Downers Grove, Ill.: InterVarsity Press, 1959) in J. S. Mill, *Nature and Utility of Religion: Two Essays*, ed. George Nakhnikian (Indianapolis, Ind.: Bobbs, 1958), p. 38.

[2]Ibid., p. 13.

[3]J. B. Phillips, *God Our Contemporary* (New York: Macmillan, 1960), pp. 88-89.

Chapter 11: Does Christianity Differ from Other World Religions?

[1]*Open Doors, 1986-1987* (New York: Institute of International Education, 1986).

Chapter 12: Is Christian Experience Valid?

[1]Anthony Standen, *Science Is a Sacred Cow* (New York: E. P. Dutton 1962), p. 25.

[2]Orville S. Walters, *You Can Win Others* (Winona Lake, Ind.: Light and Life

Press, 1950), n.p.

[3]D. Martyn Lloyd-Jones, *Conversions: Psychological or Spiritual* (Downers Grove, Ill.: InterVarsity Press, 1959), p. 13.

[4]J. B. Phillips, *God Our Contemporary* (New York: Macmillan, 1960), pp. 22-23.

[5]For an expansion of these experiences and their relevancy to life, see the author's *How to Give Away Your Faith* (Chicago: InterVarsity Press, 1966), pp. 83ff.

[6]Donald M. MacKay, *Christianity in a Mechanistic Universe* (London: Inter-Varsity Fellowship, 1965), pp. 57-59.